The Modern Pantry Cookbook

ANNA HANSEN

The MODERN PANTRY

COOKBOOK

EBURY PRESS

10 9 8 7 6 5 4 3 2 1

Published in 2011 by Ebury Press, an imprint of Ebury Publishing

A Random House Group Company

Text © Anna Hansen 2011
Photography © Christopher Terry 2011

The cover quote from Fergus Henderson is taken from *Coco*, published by
Phaidon Press Limited © 2009 Phaidon Press Limited, www.phaidon.com

The Random House Group Limited Reg. No. 954009

Addresses for companies within the Random House Group can be
found at www.randomhouse.co.uk

A CIP catalogue record for this book is available from the British Library

The Random House Group Limited supports The Forest Stewardship
Council (FSC), the leading international forest certification organisation.
All our titles that are printed on Greenpeace approved FSC certified
paper carry the FSC logo. Our paper procurement policy can be found
at www.randomhouse.co.uk/environment

To buy books by your favourite authors and register for offers visit
www.randomhouse.co.uk

Colour separations by XY Digital

Printed and bound in China by C & C Offset Printing Co., Ltd

Design: Hyperkit
Photography: Christopher Terry
Prop styling: Penny Markham
Production: David Brimble

ISBN 9780091937973

Dedicated to my Mum and my Aunty
– Mette Hansen and Kimmi Dejgaard

Contents

SNACKS AND SMALL PLATES

SALADS

VEGETABLE DISHES

SEAFOOD

POULTRY AND MEAT

DESERTS

BREAD AND BAKING

INTRODUCTION

I was born in Canada but moved to Auckland, New Zealand, when I was very young. I grew up there with my Mum's side of the family, who are Danish. As children, we were regular little hunter–gatherers. We caught eel and collected buckets of crayfish from the stream in the local pony club. We sipped nectar from the honeysuckle flowers and ate the tender stems of young, flax-like plants that seemed to grow everywhere and tasted like green apples. At the beach, we plucked and ate mussels and oysters straight from the exposed rocks, and dug for pipi, a variety of shellfish, at low tide. We would lug home anything we couldn't eat in situ, although on many occasions our catch escaped before we managed to get it into the pot or on to the barbecue.

My Dad's side of the family were dairy farmers, who lived on the Hauraki Plains, south of Auckland. My grandparents had an impressive vegetable patch and a large orchard, the fruits from which my Granny turned into the most delicious tarts, jams and preserves – all served with fresh cream, of course. They also kept chickens, whose eggs were a standard for breakfast, accompanied by enormous mushrooms picked in the paddocks. During the game season, we ate plenty of duck and pheasant, which we learned to gut and pluck ourselves.

All these gastronomic experiences were truly wonderful – extraordinary even, in the light of my current urban existence – but the greatest culinary influence in my life was my Danish grandmother, my Mormor, who lived just down the road from us in Auckland. During my childhood, I spent many happy hours in her kitchen, chatting with her and watching her prepare the daily meals, helping where I could. Some of them were elaborate affairs but most were simple.

The thing that impressed me was that whatever she was cooking, Mormor always strove for perfection. Her cuisine was typically 'immigrant' and she was skilled at adapting a recipe by replacing unavailable ingredients with something local. Her understanding of and respect for an ingredient's flavour was impressive.

When I was sixteen, my family moved to Nelson in the north of the South Island of New Zealand, where my divine uncle lived. He, too, was an exemplary cook. There I met a wonderful woman by the name of Jill Stevenson, who had opened The Hardy Street Delicatessen & Catering Company. Jill employed me as a shop assistant and kitchen hand and I worked there after school and on Saturdays. She was (and still is) an incredibly talented chef, capable of effortlessly (or so it appeared to me) creating vast and beautiful feasts for her grateful clients. She had so much energy and natural flair that I aspired to be part of that world, and soon became very good at arranging watercress around voluptuous displays of cooked hams and cream cheese logs, pronouncing exotic names and, of course, peeling potatoes and washing dishes. After much debate, though, my mother managed to persuade me that I shouldn't pursue a chef's apprenticeship just yet and that I should finish school. As she saw it, I was too young to become a chef. It was a very physically demanding job, the hours were long and antisocial and I would never see my friends – a very important consideration for a 16-year-old!

Six years later, after gaining a Diploma in Business Management and travelling in Canada for a while, I ended up in the UK. I'd had absolutely no intention of ever coming here, let alone staying, as

I had a preconceived notion that England was a miserable place where it always rained and got dark early and that London was in fact an extension of hell! But a friend convinced me to come and, in retrospect, that was a fortuitous day. Shortly afterwards, I met Tristram, brother of Margot Clayton, who was then girlfriend (now wife) of Fergus Henderson. They, with Jon Spiteri, had just opened the now-famous French House Dining Room. I needed a job and they needed a dish washer.

What an education! Fresh herbs, salads and vegetables I had never seen or even heard of before; beautiful fresh whole fish; birds and beasts that arrived in varying states of preparedness; cheeses and other wonderful ingredients. Far from being in hell, I was in heaven. Joanna Williams, another of the world's wonderful chefs and now a great friend, also worked there and she encouraged me to get involved in any way I could. Soon I was making the bread and sharpening my knife skills, and when Joanna left a few months later, Margot and Fergus offered to train me.

My Mormor always said that anyone with all the right ingredients in front of them could cook well but to be a great cook required the skill of being able to create something delicious, even splendid, out of very humble ingredients. I think this is why I so greatly appreciated Margot and Fergus's approach to food. Their philosophy of unadulterated flavours and textures no matter how humble the fixings was inspiring.

Then I met Peter Gordon, soon to be of Sugar Club fame, the boldest and most creative chef I have ever known. Peter's approach to food was truly unique, and the polar opposite of Fergus and Margot's. His impact on my development as a chef was vast. He taught me to experiment and not to be afraid to try what then seemed to me outlandish combinations. He impressed on me the importance of keeping a completely open mind – a lesson to which I attribute my creativity.

Since then, I have worked with many talented chefs here in the UK, and in New Zealand and Australia. I have also travelled here and there around the world. Together with Peter and our partners, I was a founding member of the award-winning Providores restaurant in London, which we opened in 2001. Then, in 2005, I set out to do my own thing and, after a three-and-a-half-year 'journey', opened The Modern Pantry, the greatest achievement in my life thus far. Housed in two beautiful, light-filled Georgian buildings in Clerkenwell, it is modern and sleek, blending traditional features with contemporary inspiration – much like the food that is created there. We serve breakfast, lunch and dinner seven days a week to whoever cares to be served and it brings me untold joy every day (as well as the occasional headache)!

The questions I am most often asked are how I came to be producing the type of cuisine I do today, how I come up with the seemingly bizarre combinations of ingredients and how I gain my inspiration. For some, in fact for many, my approach to cooking and the combinations I create appear quite unusual, yet to me they all seem perfectly natural and possess a certain logic. Like all chefs, I focus on creating dishes whose flavours and textures are complementary and balanced (while hoping that they also happen to look good). But unlike many chefs, I am not concerned with the origins of each ingredient, in the sense

that I do not let its origins dictate how I choose to cook it or with what I choose to serve it. For me, a spoonful of Japanese miso is just as welcome in a classic French celeriac remoulade as Dijon mustard. And why not? It is just another form of seasoning, another condiment from another part of the world designed for the same purpose: to enhance flavour. My larder is global. There are no culinary boundaries in my kitchen.

The recipes you'll find in this book are a reflection of this philosophy and I hope they will inspire you to approach the contents of your pantry with a more open mind. There are some unusual ingredients and some of the recipes may seem a little long, but please don't be put off. You will be surprised what you can find locally or online if you take the time to look. And if there is an ingredient you cannot find, why not take the opportunity to have some fun experimenting? To me that is what cooking is all about.

I have chosen my favourite recipes to appear here – recipes that are fresh, simple and full of sensational flavours. Some are now staples at The Modern Pantry and some are dishes I like to cook at home. Regardless, they are all recipes that I think will shine in your hands while at the same time showing you how easy it is to think creatively with food. They are everyday recipes fused with modern ingredients. Welcome to my pantry!

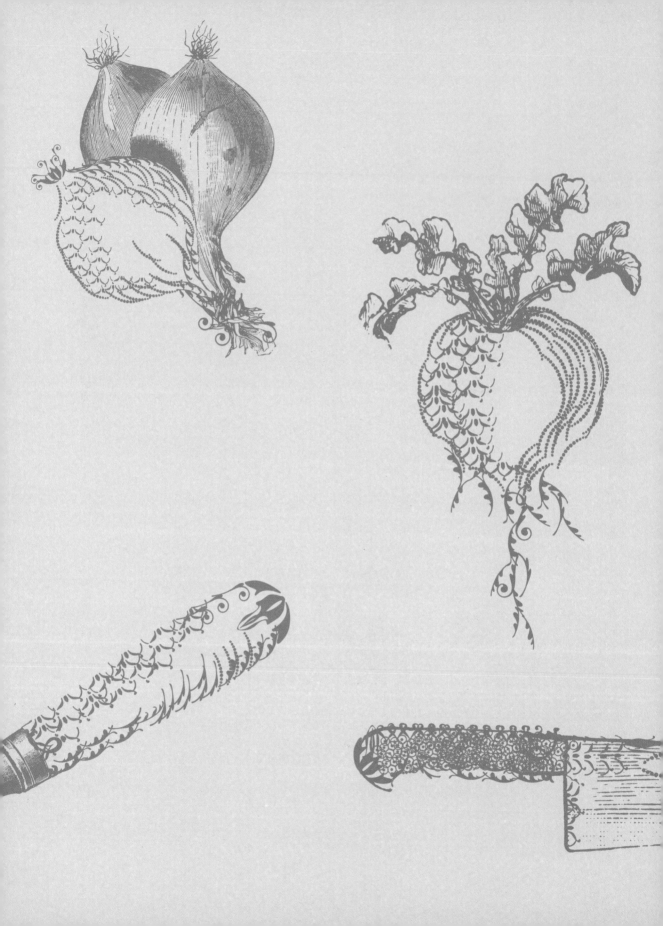

CONDIMENTS

SMOKED CHILLI SAMBAL

I first learned about this versatile Southeast-Asian preparation from my great friend and fellow chef, Gianni Vatteroni, in the days of The Sugar Club restaurant. It has endless incarnations and can include many other flavourings and spices. You can store it in the fridge for several months or freeze it.

Heat some oil to 180°C in a deep-fat fryer or a large, deep pan, then deep-fry the red peppers, onions and tomatoes separately in small batches until they are a deep golden brown – almost burnt looking. Drain them on kitchen paper and then tip them into a large bowl as you go. Deep-fry the ginger and garlic, in separate batches also, until just golden brown.

In a small frying pan, fry the ground shrimps in a little of the oil from the fryer until aromatic. Add them to the bowl along with all the remaining ingredients and mix thoroughly.

Now blitz the sambal in batches in a food processor until almost smooth, emptying it out into another bowl as you go. Once you have done this, mix the processed sambal together thoroughly and allow to cool. Place in an airtight container and refrigerate until needed.

MAKES ABOUT 1KG
rapeseed oil for deep-frying
250g red peppers, sliced
250g onions, sliced
250g ripe cherry tomatoes
80g fresh ginger, cut into
    fine strips
80g garlic, sliced
25g dried shrimps, ground
    finely in a spice grinder
1 tsp chipotle chilli flakes
    (or 1 tsp hot smoked
    paprika)
¼ tsp dried chilli flakes
125g tamarind paste
40ml fish sauce (nam pla)

LAKSA PASTE

Don't be put off by the large amount this recipe makes. It keeps in the fridge for several weeks if stored in an airtight container, covered in a light film of oil, or you can freeze it in small batches for up to six months, ready to use when the mood takes you.

Toast the coriander seeds, cumin seeds, star anise and cinnamon stick in a dry frying pan over a moderate heat until aromatic, then grind in a spice grinder or using a pestle and mortar.

Place in a food processor, add all the remaining ingredients except the oil, then blitz to a paste, adding the oil a little at a time as necessary to aid the process. Store in the fridge, covered with a thin layer of oil, or freeze.

MAKES ABOUT 750G
2 tbsp coriander seeds
2 tbsp cumin seeds
8 star anise
1 cinnamon stick
65g green chillies,
    roughly chopped
100g peeled garlic
175g peeled fresh ginger,
    roughly chopped
150g peeled fresh galangal,
    roughly chopped
7 lemongrass stalks,
    trimmed and sliced
15 kaffir lime leaves
a large bunch of
    coriander stalks
about 150ml vegetable oil

CRISPY SHALLOTS

I know, deep-frying is taboo. But sometimes one has to make the sacrifice in order to produce a delectable morsel. If you don't have the time or the inclination to make your own perfectly crispy shallots, you could of course drop by your local Asian store and pick some up for a song, but for me, making my own always gives me a bit of a thrill. They taste infinitesimally better, and it is so easy to make them that it seems a shame to miss an opportunity to pat oneself on the back!

I prefer to use rapeseed oil for deep-frying. It has a higher burning tolerance and is easy to find wherever you shop.

Using a mandoline or a very sharp knife, slice the shallots into fine rounds. Pour the oil into a deep pan or a deep-fat fryer, add the shallots and turn on to a moderate heat. Gradually the shallots will begin to fry. If you happen to have such gadgets in your house, find your cooking thermometer and do not let the heat of the oil exceed 160°C. If you don't have a thermometer, just make sure the flame is at a medium pace. Stir the shallots from time to time. This is important, as heat is never constant in a pan and you need to make sure the shallots are cooking evenly. They are done when they are golden and are not bubbling particularly frantically, which indicates that most of the moisture they naturally retain has evaporated. This will probably take about 5 minutes.

Remove the shallots with a slotted spoon, place on kitchen paper and toss around a bit to ensure that the excess oil has been thoroughly absorbed. Allow to cool, then store in an airtight container lined with fresh kitchen paper until ready to use.

4 banana shallots, peeled
1 litre rapeseed oil

DEN MISO

I manage to use this Japanese condiment one way or another almost daily at The Modern Pantry, and you'll find I've used in several recipes in this book. It is a great standby to have up your sleeve and lasts for up to three months in an airtight container in the fridge, so you'll have plenty of time to use it up.

Place all the ingredients in a pan and whisk over a medium heat until dissolved. Cool and store in an airtight container in the fridge.

MAKES ABOUT 1 LITRE
100ml sake
100ml mirin
600g white miso
300g white sugar

MARINATED FETA

I love marinated feta, with its surprising burst of some spice or other against a salty, creamy backdrop. It spruces up any dish calling for feta and is so simple, tasty and versatile that it is a crime not to have any in your fridge. Try crumbling some into warm lentils just before you serve them. You could also experiment with different combinations of herbs and toasted spices.

Put 75ml of the oil in a small pan over a moderate heat. Add the curry leaves, fennel, caraway and black mustard seeds and the Urfa chilli flakes and fry for a minute or so, until aromatic. Remove from the heat and leave to cool.

Pour the cooled spiced oil over the feta along with the remaining 50ml of oil. Gently toss the feta in the oil and then refrigerate in an airtight container until ready to use.

SERVES 8 WHEN USED
IN A SALAD
125ml Confit Artichoke oil
    (see page 128) or extra
    virgin olive oil
10 curry leaves
½ tsp fennel seeds
½ tsp caraway seeds
½ tsp black mustard seeds
½ tsp Urfa chilli flakes
300g feta cheese, cut into
    1cm cubes
5 basil leaves, shredded

TURMERIC AND CARDAMOM PICKLED LOTUS ROOT

Over the years I think I have pretty much tried to pickle most fruit and vegetables, not to mention fish and meat. Pickles are so versatile and once you have mastered the basics – and they are very basic – you can have endless fun experimenting with different flavour combinations.

This recipe uses a simple rule of thumb that I generally adhere to for vegetables and fruit: one part vinegar to two parts water. You can then add sugar, salt or spices to taste, or try different vinegars, sugars and so on. Things we pickle regularly at The Modern Pantry include beansprouts, cucumber, beetroot, rhubarb, plums and grapes.

If you don't want to pickle the whole lotus root in this recipe, you can freeze some for a rainy day or slice it thinly on a mandoline and fry until golden. Dust the lotus root 'crisps' with icing sugar and serve as a decoration for a dessert, or sprinkle them with fine sea salt and serve alongside the pickled lotus root for a contrasting texture and colour. They look beautiful together.

Also try adding thinly sliced raw beetroot to the pickling liquid instead of turmeric – the beetroot will dye the lotus root, or whatever you are pickling for that matter, red.

Peel the lotus root, slice finely on a mandoline and place in a large container with a lid. Put all the remaining ingredients into a pan and bring to the boil, stirring occasionally to dissolve the sugar. Reduce the heat and leave to simmer for 3–4 minutes, then pour it over the lotus root. Allow to cool, then refrigerate until ready to use. The pickled lotus root will keep for up to a month in the fridge.

1 lotus root
6 cardamom pods,
   lightly crushed
1¼ tsp finely grated
   fresh turmeric
   (or ¾ tsp ground turmeric)
400ml rice wine vinegar
   or cider vinegar
800ml water
220g white sugar
1 tbsp salt

PICKLED WATERMELON RIND

I love all Jane Grigson's food but this is my favourite of her recipes.
It puts to excellent use all those watermelon rinds one generally
discards over the summer months. Wonderful with cheese and
cold cuts or added to a salad.

Scoop any flesh from the rind of your watermelon, leaving a
thin layer of pink, and place the rind in a bowl. Make a brine
by dissolving 2 level tablespoons of salt in every litre of water,
making enough to cover your rind. Submerge the rind in it and
leave for 24 hours. Drain the rind, rinse under cold water, then
simmer in a pan of fresh water until tender.

Put the pickling ingredients in another large pan and bring
to the boil, stirring to dissolve the sugar. Reduce the heat
and add the watermelon rind. Simmer until it looks candied,
approximately 40 minutes. Bottle in sterilised jars and store
for a month before using.

MAKES 1KG
1kg watermelon rind
salt

For the pickling liquid:
1kg white sugar
500ml water
500ml cider vinegar
1 lemon, thinly sliced
1 cinnamon stick
1 tsp cloves
2 star anise

SAFFRON AND CARAWAY PICKLED RHUBARB

This pickle is a delicious, aromatic accompaniment to roast lamb or
pork, but is also great served on a cheese plate or tossed through a salad.
Try it with the the roast cod dish on page 152.

Split the rhubarb stalks lengthwise and cut into 2.5cm lengths.
Place in a storage container just large enough to hold them.

Bring the remaining ingredients to the boil in a pan, reduce
the heat and simmer for 5 minutes. Pour this mixture over
the rhubarb and leave to cool. Cover and store in the fridge
until ready to use. The pickled rhubarb should keep for about
two months.

MAKES ABOUT 2L
600g rhubarb
300ml rice wine vinegar
600ml water
175g white sugar
1 tsp caraway seeds
a pinch of saffron strands
1 tbsp pomegranate molasses
1 tsp Maldon salt or other
    flaky sea salt

SUE'S 15-MINUTE PRESERVED LEMONS

Oh, the joy of a preserved lemon. I love the whole romance of making them, I have to say. The quartering of the lemon almost to the base and then stuffing it with salt, the hunt for accommodating jars to prod them into and then the squeezing of untold additional lemons until your hands are screaming out, in order to provide the juice to make it all work. Beautiful. And then the wait – a month minimum, but if you are to do them justice, at least two.

And where can you buy a decent preserved lemon in the Western world? I don't think you can, or at least I have never come across one, and either way they cost a fortune so best to make your own.

And so your lemons are brewing but you need some now. Stage right, enter Sue Lewis with her magical 15-minute preserved lemon recipe! Don't stop making your own according to the traditional method but this recipe is genius. You don't get the same texture as you would by finely dicing those beautifully aged lemon rinds but you do get the lemony, salty hit you hope for from a preserved lemon and the best thing is you can make it in 15 minutes.

Place all the ingredients in a small pan over a low heat and bring to the boil. Leave to simmer gently for about 10 minutes, until the lemon zest is tender. Remove from the heat, cool and then store in the fridge until needed.

zest of 4 lemons, pared
   off with a potato peeler
the juice of the 4 lemons
1 tsp Maldon salt or
   other flaky sea salt

Et voilà!

TOMATILLO CHILLI JAM

This recipe is a remake of the classic tomato chilli jam, so it works just as well with tomatoes and is especially good with green ones. Use as you would any relish or jam of this nature.

Place all the ingredients in a shallow pan and bring to the boil. Reduce the heat, skim off any foam that has risen to the surface and simmer gently for approximately 40 minutes, until thick and glossy. Transfer to sterilised jars and seal. The jam can be used immediately or stored for up to a year.

MAKES ABOUT 2L

1.5kg tomatillos, husks
   removed, roughly chopped
5 star anise
1 cinnamon stick
4 cardamom pods,
   lightly crushed
3 green chillies, finely
   sliced into rounds
4 garlic cloves, finely sliced
1 large thumb-sized piece
   of fresh ginger, cut into
   fine strips
400g white sugar
300ml cider vinegar

GREEN PEPPER AND APPLE RELISH

There are few foods that I dislike on this planet, at least that I have tried thus far, but I have to admit that green peppers are up there, headlining for kidneys and durian. Whether they are served raw or cooked, I find they taste rather like dirt, and who wants to eat dirt other than perhaps a worm? But then there is this Green Pepper and Apple Relish, the one and only exception I make in my otherwise green-pepperless life. It couldn't be easier to make and it goes with just about anything.

Blitz the peppers, apples, ginger and onions in a food processor to achieve a rough paste. Tip into a heavy-bottomed pan and add all the remaining ingredients. Bring to the boil, skim off any foam that has risen to the surface, then reduce the heat to a gentle simmer. Cook, stirring frequently, for 40 minutes or until a jammy consistency has been reached. Place in an airtight container, or bottle, if you like, and store in your fridge.

MAKES ABOUT 2 JARS

500g green peppers, deseeded
300g cored apples, cut into quarters
50g fresh ginger, roughly chopped
125g onions, roughly chopped
20g garlic, sliced
2 green chillies, thinly sliced into rounds
175ml cider vinegar
75ml fish sauce (nam pla)
250g white sugar

TOMATO RELISH

This is one of my favourite relish recipes and finds its way into many dishes at The Modern Pantry. You could try adding a spoonful or two to cooked lentils or to finish a tomato curry.

Heat the oil in a heavy-bottomed pan and fry the cumin and mustard seeds, ginger, chillies and turmeric until aromatic. Add all the remaining ingredients, bring to the boil and skim off any foam that has arisen. Reduce the heat to a gentle simmer and cook gently for 40 minutes or so, until thick and shiny. Remove from the heat, cool and bottle, or store in an airtight container in your fridge.

MAKES ABOUT 2 JARS
2 tbsp vegetable oil
1 tbsp cumin seeds,
    toasted in a dry frying
    pan and then ground
3 tsp yellow mustard seeds
80g fresh ginger, finely
    chopped
2 red chillies, finely chopped
20g fresh turmeric,
    finely grated
2 400g cans of chopped
    tomatoes
150ml white wine vinegar
    or cider vinegar
40g palm sugar
    (if you can't get any,
    substitute demerara)
40ml fish sauce (nam pla)

COX'S APPLE, SOUR CHERRY AND FENNEL CHUTNEY

This chutney is delicious with roast pork or a good Cheddar and some homemade oatcakes (see page 215).

Put everything in a roasting dish, cover with foil and place in an oven preheated to 160°C/Gas Mark 3. Cook for 1 hour, stirring once or twice, then remove the foil and continue to cook for 30–40 minutes. The chutney should be glossy and slightly caramelised, with a nice syrupy consistency. Cook for longer if necessary.

Remove from the oven and leave to cool. Spoon into sterilised jars, cover and refrigerate. It will last for several months in the fridge.

MAKES ABOUT 2 JARS

90g dried sour cherries, soaked overnight in apple juice

1kg Cox's apples, peeled, cored and roughly chopped

2 fennel bulbs, finely sliced across (a mandoline is very good for this)

1 red onion, cut in half and sliced lengthways, from the root end to the top

100g fresh ginger, finely grated

1 red chilli, finely sliced into rings

2 tsp fennel seeds

2 tsp coriander seeds

3 star anise

250g demerara sugar

400ml cider vinegar

DARK CHICKEN STOCK

This is the only dark stock we make at The Modern Pantry and the only one I ever make at home. Rich and tasty, it is the perfect all-rounder.

Put the chicken carcasses or pieces in a roasting tin and roast in an oven preheated to 180°C/Gas Mark 4 until thoroughly golden.

Meanwhile, heat the oil in a pan large enough to hold the chicken and vegetables with a good few centimetres to spare. Add the carrots, celery, onions, garlic and leek and sauté over a high heat for about 10 minutes, until browned. Add the herbs, fennel seeds and peppercorns and the roasted chicken.

Deglaze the hot roasting tin by pouring in half the red wine and stirring to scrape up all the caramelised goodies that have stuck to the tray (avoid any burnt bits, as they will make the stock bitter). Add this liquid to the pan, then pour in enough water to come at least 5cm above the bones. Slowly bring to a simmer over a moderate heat, skimming off any scum that rises to the surface, then reduce the heat to the gentlest of simmers.

Leave the stock to cook very gently for 5 hours, regularly skimming off the fat and other impurities. Do not let it boil, as this will result in a cloudy, fatty stock.

Remove from the heat and leave to stand in a cool place for 30 minutes or so, then strain, first through a colander and then through a fine sieve into another pan. Add the remaining red wine and cook at a rapid simmer until reduced by half. Remove from the heat, leave to cool and then store in the fridge until ready to use. If I do not need all of the stock, I freeze it in ice-cube trays, then turn it out into a freezer bag or container and keep frozen until required.

MAKES ABOUT 1 LITRE

2.5kg chicken carcasses,
  or a whole chicken, jointed
2 tbsp vegetable oil
3 carrots, peeled and
  roughly chopped
3 celery sticks, roughly
  chopped
2 onions, quartered
  (leave the skin on)
2 heads of garlic,
  halved widthways
1 large leek, roughly chopped
a bunch of parsley stalks
½ bunch of thyme
½ bunch of rosemary
6 bay leaves
1 tbsp fennel seeds
2 tsp black peppercorns
500ml red wine

PRAWN OIL

This crustacean oil is a byproduct of making the Sugar-cured Prawn Omelette on page 58, or any other prawn dish for that matter, and is a fantastic way of using up the shells. I love it, and it is so simple to make. If you have only a few shells, freeze them until you have enough. You could also use other crustacean shells, such as crab or lobster. If using either of the latter, I highly recommend smashing them up a bit before roasting, in order to maximise the flavour.

The oil has a two-week shelf life in the fridge but you can also freeze it in an ice-cube tray and later tip the cubes out into a freezer bag so that you have it to hand any time. Use it for frying fish or for adding a burst of crustacean goodness to a crab or lobster salad dressing.

MAKES ABOUT 1 LITRE

2 banana shallots, diced
2 lemongrass stalks, trimmed, bashed and chopped
a 50g knob of fresh ginger, finely sliced
4 garlic cloves, peeled
a pinch of saffron strands (optional)
600g prawn shells
vegetable oil, to cover

Put the shallots, lemongrass, ginger, garlic and saffron, if you are using it, in a roasting or casserole dish that is just large enough to hold the prawn shells snugly. You could use a small casserole if you don't have a small enough dish. Place the shells on top of the shallot mixture and barely cover with oil.

Place the dish in an oven preheated to 140°C/Gas Mark 1 and bake for 1 hour. Remove from the oven and leave to cool slightly, then strain through a fine-meshed sieve into a sterilised jar and store for .

PRAWN STOCK

Another great way of using leftover prawn shells is to make a stock.
Excellent to have on hand for making laksas or other fish-based soups,
and I also use it in the Singapore-style Wokked Crab on page 156.
Again, you can use any other crustacean shells you may have.

Heat the vegetable oil in a large pan, add the shallots, garlic
and ginger and fry over a moderate heat until beginning to
soften. Add the celery, carrots, lemongrass and lime leaves and
continue to cook for 5 minutes or so, stirring from time to time.
Add the prawn shells and cook gently for 5 minutes, then pour
in the white wine and enough water barely to cover. Bring to the
boil, reduce the heat to a gentle simmer and skim off any foam
that has risen to the surface. Simmer for 30 minutes.

Remove from the heat and leave to cool almost completely,
then strain through a fine-meshed sieve, gently pushing down
on the shells to extract as much of the broth as possible. Store
in the fridge for up to two days or freeze for a rainy day.

MAKES ABOUT 1.5 LITRES
2 tbsp vegetable oil
3 banana shallots, finely sliced
2 garlic cloves, finely sliced
a thumb-sized knob of fresh
  ginger, finely sliced
1 celery stick, finely sliced
2 carrots, finely sliced
2 lemongrass stalks, trimmed,
  bashed and chopped
4 kaffir lime leaves
600g prawn shells
150ml white wine

SOY-BRAISED HIJIKI

We always have a stash of this in our fridge and you will be amazed what you can do with it once you put your mind to it. We use it in soups, salads, stews, lentils, tortillas – the list goes on.

Place all the ingredients in a pan, bring to the boil, then reduce the heat and simmer for about 20 minutes, until the hijiki is tender. Cool and store in an airtight container in the fridge for up to a month.

MAKES ABOUT 500ML
20g dried hijiki seaweed
125ml light soy sauce
125ml mirin
250ml water

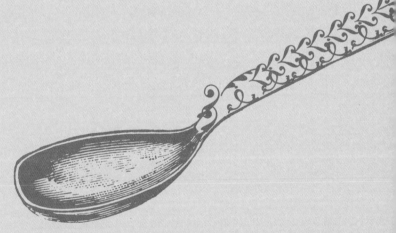

BREAKFAST
AND BRUNCH

Passion Fruit and Banana Smoothie

For me smoothies are synonymous with brunch and the recipes on this page and the opposite one are a couple of combinations that I particularly like. The possibilities are endless however and as long as you have some flavoursome fruit, a little yoghurt (although even this element is optional!) and some ice you are on your way! A liquidiser also helps but a food processor or hand blender will be fine.

Put all the ingredients in a liquidiser and blend until smooth. Add more lemon juice to taste, if necessary, and a little water if the mixture is too thick. Serve immediately.

Serves 2

250g Greek yoghurt
1 ripe banana
125ml passion fruit purée
  (you can buy this, or use
  the pulp and seeds of ripe
  passion fruit)
15–20 ice cubes
  depending on the
  size of the cube
juice of ½ lemon

Lychee, Raspberry and Rose Smoothie

If you are unable to find fresh lychees, you may substitute canned ones but they will be sweeter, so be sure to balance the acidity with more lemon juice.

You may need a little more rosewater, depending on the strength of the brand you have, but I urge you to add it cautiously! Too much will make your smoothie overly perfumed and cloying.

Put all the ingredients in a liquidiser and blend until smooth. Add more lemon juice to taste, if necessary, and a little water if the mixture is too thick. Serve immediately.

Serves 2
250g Greek yoghurt
130g fresh or frozen raspberries
130g fresh lychees, stones removed
2 tsp rosewater
15–20 ice cubes depending on the size of the cube
juice of ½ lemon

HONEY-ROASTED OATS, SEEDS AND NUTS

For those of you who don't make your own granola, I have one question
… why not? Not only is it super easy to make, its flavour is, I think, vastly
superior to pretty much any shop-bought variety. This recipe is really
just a guide to get you started – you can experiment and add or remove
dried fruits, nuts and grains as you see fit.

At The Modern Pantry we like to serve it with grated apple or
pear mixed through and natural yoghurt.

Gently heat the honey, oil and sugar in a pan, simmer until the
sugar has dissolved, then set aside to cool. Mix the remaining
ingredients together in a bowl, pour over the honey mixture
and thoroughly stir it all together.

Divide the mixture between two parchment-lined baking trays
and spread evenly. Bake in an oven preheated to 160°C/Gas
Mark 3 for 20 minutes or so, stirring from time to time to ensure
even baking. When the mixture is golden, remove the trays from
the oven and leave to cool. Store in an airtight container for up
to one month.

MAKES ABOUT 1KG
75g honey
60ml extra virgin olive oil
40g light soft brown sugar
250g rolled oats
250g jumbo oats
50g desiccated coconut
75g hazelnuts, toasted
   and lightly crushed
140g pumpkin seeds
140g sunflower seeds
1 tbsp black sesame seeds
1 tbsp white sesame seeds

BANANA AND CHOCOLATE MUFFINS

What could be better than a freshly baked muffin with your smoothie and perfectly brewed cup of coffee in the morning? Wonderfully moist and fluffy, these muffins are a winner. Banana and chocolate chip is a flavour combination that I am a fan of but the brilliance of this recipe is that you can chop and change flavours to suit your tastes and what is in your pantry. Just stick to the measurements given below and you can't go wrong.

Whisk the oil, buttermilk and egg together in a large bowl. Sift the flour, sugar and salt on top of this and fold through until the mixture is just beginning to form a paste. Add the diced banana and chocolate chips and gently fold through – the secret of success with these muffins is not to overmix.

Divide the mixture between six muffin cases in a muffin tin, place a banana slice on top of each one and push it into the batter a little. This is just to make sure it stays in place whilst cooking, not to hide it in the batter! Sprinkle with demerara sugar and bake in an oven preheated to 180°C/Gas Mark 4 for 20 minutes or until a skewer inserted in the centre comes out clean. Remove from the oven and leave to cool. The muffins are best eaten on the day they are made, still warm even, but they will keep for a couple of days in an airtight container.

SERVES 6
50ml vegetable oil
150ml buttermilk
   (or 150ml yoghurt,
   thinned with a little water)
1 egg
180g self-raising flour
90g caster sugar
¼ tsp salt
150g banana flesh, diced,
   plus 6 slices of banana
60g dark chocolate chips
demerara sugar for sprinkling

Elderflower-poached Tamarillos

I grew up in New Zealand, where the tamarillo, or tree tomato as it is also known, was a pretty everyday event when in season. It seemed that everyone had a tamarillo tree (although we didn't!) and we cut the fruit in half, maybe sprinkling them with a little sugar, and scooped out the bitter-sweet flesh with a spoon. At least that is what the adults did. I seem to recall just biting them in half and squeezing the pulp out into my mouth with my fingers, barbaric child that I was.

Although tamarillos are not that easy to come by in the UK (though you can find them in large supermarkets and specialist fruit and vegetable shops), I feel compelled to include them in this book. They are always on the breakfast menu at The Modern Pantry.

You can make up the elderflower poaching liquor to use as the base of a refreshing spritzer. Pour a few shots into a glass, add plenty of ice and top up with soda water or sparkling water and a squeeze of lemon or lime juice.

Bring the sugar, wine, water, lemon zest and juice and the star anise to the boil in a pan, stirring to dissolve the sugar. Reduce the heat to a gentle simmer and drop in the elderflower heads. Let this poaching liquor simmer gently for 5 minutes, then remove from the heat and leave to steep until the liquid is tepid. Strain the liquor through a fine-meshed sieve, pushing down on the elderflowers with the back of a ladle or spoon to extract as much flavour as possible. Return the liquor to the pan

Using a serrated knife or a sharp paring knife, very lightly score a cross at the tip of each tamarillo to reach a quarter of the way down the side of the fruit. Be careful not to cut into the flesh, or the fruit will disintegrate during cooking. This process is to enable you to remove the skin easily after poaching.

Add the tamarillos to the poaching liquor in the pan and bring to the boil. Remove from the heat immediately and leave the fruit to cool in the liquor. When cool, gently peel the skin from the fruit, then return them to the poaching liquor. Store in the fridge until ready to serve.

Serves 6
400g granulated sugar
500ml white wine
500ml water
zest of 2 lemons, removed
   with a potato peeler
juice of 1 lemon
4 star anise
6 elderflower heads
6 tamarillos

Coconut Waffles with Vanilla Mascarpone, Mango and Passion Fruit

Waffles are one of all-time my favourite things, especially for brunch. For a variation, replace the desiccated coconut with polenta and serve with bacon and maple syrup.

I'm afraid you'll need a waffle iron to make this recipe.

To make the vanilla mascarpone, put the mascarpone into a bowl and loosen it with a whisk. Add the double cream and some vanilla sugar and whisk until lump free, thick and glossy.

To make the waffles, sift the flour, sugar and salt into a bowl and stir in the desiccated coconut. Gently whisk in the water, beer, whipped cream, melted butter and egg yolks. In a separate bowl, whisk the egg whites until they form soft peaks and then fold them through the batter, being careful not to overmix.

To cook the waffles, heat your waffle iron and brush it lightly with butter. Spoon in some of the batter and spread it almost to the edge of the waffle pattern, then close the lid and cook until golden. This should take 4 minutes or so. The amount of batter you need will depend on the depth of your iron so play around until you get the volume right. This recipe makes 10–12 waffles. You will want more than one!

To serve, place a waffle or two on each plate and dust with icing sugar. Put a spoonful of the mascarpone cream on top, place a few pieces of mango on this and then drizzle over the passion fruit pulp.

Serves 6

For the waffles:
270g plain flour
2 tbsp sugar
¼ tsp salt
100g desiccated coconut
200ml tepid water
200ml tepid beer or ale
150ml double cream, lightly whipped
100g unsalted butter, melted, plus extra for brushing
4 eggs, separated

For the topping:
icing sugar for dusting
2 ripe mangoes, peeled with a potato peeler, then sliced into generous chunks
pulp of 6 passion fruit

For the vanilla mascarpone:
150g mascarpone cheese
150ml double cream
vanilla sugar, to taste

JERUSALEM ARTICHOKE AND TALEGGIO TORTILLA

I have been making tortillas (or frittatas, as we call them in New Zealand, where they are a requirement on the café circuit) since my student days. They were a staple when I was studying, usually involving cheap canned sardines and even cheaper cheese. Brain food and protein – perfect! These days I try to be a bit more sophisticated about my choice of ingredients but in reality most things taste great with eggs, so pretty much anything goes.

The best thing about a tortilla is that it tastes even better the following day so it's an excellent choice for a hassle-free brunch or tapas with that well-deserved glass of wine at the end of the day.

This recipe is just a guide and you must feel free to make substitutes for any or all of the ingredients, except the eggs, of course. Try roast sweet potatoes or parsnips or a blue cheese for something truly decadent.

Toss the Jerusalem artichokes with a little olive oil, season lightly and roast in an oven preheated to 180°C/Gas Mark 4 for 20 minutes or so, until tender and beginning to caramelise. Remove from the oven but leave it on.

Heat 2 tablespoons of olive oil in a frying pan, add the onion and fry over a moderate heat for 3–4 minutes. Add the garlic, ginger and thyme and continue to fry until the onion is soft and beginning to colour. Remove from the heat and add the parsley, spring onions and hijiki.

Whisk the eggs in a large bowl. Add the Taleggio, along with the Jerusalem artichokes, the onion mixture and ⅓ teaspoon each of salt and pepper. Mix thoroughly but gently.

Heat 4 tablespoons of olive oil in a large, heavy ovenproof frying pan until smoking. It may seem a lot of oil but don't skimp, as it is going to ensure (I hope!) that your beautiful tortilla comes easily from the pan once cooked. Pour in the egg mixture and allow it to bubble for 30 seconds or so, then shake the pan as you would a wok, gently flipping the contents so that the cooked egg on the bottom rotates to the top. Transfer the pan to the oven and bake for 15–20 minutes. You don't want the egg to soufflé and become aerated, so keep an eye on its progress. It is cooked when the egg is just on the verge of setting.

Remove from the oven and leave to sit for 5 minutes or so, then carefully invert on to a plate. Serve at your leisure.

SERVES 6
500g Jerusalem artichokes, peeled and cut into 2cm dice
olive oil
1 large onion, finely sliced
3 garlic cloves, finely sliced
1 thumb-sized knob of fresh ginger, finely chopped
1 tbsp chopped thyme
½ bunch of flat-leaf parsley, chopped
6 spring onions, finely sliced
2 tbsp Soy-braised Hijiki, drained (see page 43)
10 eggs
150g Taleggio cheese, diced
Maldon salt or other flaky sea salt
black pepper

Ricotta, Sweetcorn and Coriander Pancakes with Avocado and Lime Pickle Purée

These pancakes are supremely light and fluffy and wonderful served with the avocado and lime pickle purée, a genius invention from one of my chefs, Lizzy Stables. They can also be served simply with soured cream and some chunks of avocado tossed with lime juice and a sprinkling of Aleppo or Urfa chilli flakes.

The batter freezes very well for up to a month. I suggest folding through a little more ricotta after defrosting.

Sift the flour, salt and sugar into a large bowl. Whisk together the egg yolks, buttermilk and melted butter and mix this into the dry ingredients. Carefully fold in the ricotta, being careful not to break it up too much, along with the corn, chilli, coriander and spring onions. In a separate bowl, whisk the egg whites to slightly firmer than soft peaks and then fold them through the batter in three batches.

Heat a little butter in an ovenproof frying pan and dollop spoonfuls of the batter into it. Put the pan into an oven preheated to 180°C/Gas Mark 4 and cook for 4 minutes or so, then remove and flip the pancakes. Return to the oven for 4 minutes or until the pancakes are cooked through and feel firm to the touch. Set aside somewhere warm while you cook the rest.

To make the pickle purée, peel and stone the avocados, cut them into chunks and purée in a food processor with the lime pickle. Check the seasoning.

Serve the pancakes warm with the avocado and lime pickle purée and some coriander leaves to garnish.

Serves 6

For the pancakes:
150g self-raising flour
1 tsp table salt
25g caster sugar
4 large eggs, separated
185ml buttermilk
65g unsalted butter, melted, plus extra for frying
375g ricotta cheese
200g fresh corn kernels (or canned or frozen corn)
1 green chilli, finely chopped
a bunch of coriander, chopped, plus extra leaves to garnish
2 spring onions, finely sliced

For the pickle purée:
3 ripe avocados
200g good-quality bought lime pickle
Maldon salt or other flaky sea salt
black pepper

GOATS' CURD PANCAKES WITH POMEGRANATE MOLASSES ROAST GRAPES

These pancakes are a sweeter version of the ones on page 55 and are equally delicious. You could substitute ordinary curd cheese or ricotta for the goats' curd.

Put the grapes in a roasting tin just large enough to hold them in a single layer. Sprinkle over the sugar, pomegranate molasses and verjus and roast in an oven preheated to 140°C/Gas Mark 1 for 15–20 minutes. The grapes should be just beginning to collapse in on themselves. Remove from the oven and leave to cool in their juices.

Cook the pancakes as described on page 55 and serve with the roast grapes, crème fraîche and a dusting of icing sugar.

SERVES 6

1 quantity of the pancake
batter on page 55,
substituting goats' curd
for the ricotta and omitting
the corn, chilli, coriander
and spring onions
butter for frying
400ml crème fraîche
icing sugar, for dusting

For the pomegranate
molasses roast grapes:
400g seedless red grapes,
stalks removed
1½ tbsp demerara sugar
3 tbsp pomegranate molasses
2 tbsp verjus

SUGAR-CURED PRAWN OMELETTE WITH SMOKED CHILLI SAMBAL

This is THE signature dish at The Modern Pantry. To me, it has the perfect balance of flavour, texture and aroma and I think it truly reflects my approach to cooking.

It began with me finding a packet of dried prawns in my pantry and then daydreaming about all the things I could do with them. I became so enthusiastic that I decided to try making my own. As you can imagine, air-drying prawns is not that easy from an urban kitchen window and, somehow, drying them in the oven felt like cheating. I moved on to the idea of sugar-curing the prawns as you would a piece of salmon or beef fillet but with an Asian influence. Hmmm. Not quite what I had hoped for. Finally I tossed them into a frying pan, where they were transformed into the delicious sweet and slightly crunchy caramelised morsels that eventually became the centrepiece of the sugar-cured prawn omelette.

Although I have put the recipe in the Breakfast and Brunch chapter of the book, this omelette really is good at any time of the day or night. We also serve it as a canapé by scrambling the eggs softly with the chilli sambal, then putting a little of the mixture in a spoon, topping with a sautéed prawn, a ring or two of green chilli and spring onion and a sprig of coriander. I would recommend using Chinese ceramic spoons for this as they have a flat bottom and thus sit happily on a serving platter but any spoon will do.

This recipe is a little time-consuming but if its popularity at the restaurant is anything to go by, it is well worth the effort. The prawns and the sambal can be made several days in advance, so there's no need to tackle it all at once.

To sugar-cure the prawns, mix all the ingredients together well, then cover and leave in the fridge to marinate for 24 hours. Rinse the prawns and pat dry. Store them in an airtight container in the fridge until ready to use. They should keep for six days.

For each omelette, whisk two eggs together in a small bowl with ⅛ teaspoon of the sambal. The sambal provides the seasoning, so avoid the urge to add salt. Heat a knob of butter in a non-stick omelette pan over a moderate heat. When it begins to sizzle, add six prawn halves. Toss these in the pan until almost cooked, then pour in the eggs. Swirl the pan once or twice, then reduce the heat and sprinkle over some green chilli rounds and a small handful of spring onion slices. When the eggs look almost

SERVES 6

To sugar-cure the prawns:

18 raw tiger prawns, peeled, cut in half lengthways and de-veined

1 lemongrass stalk, trimmed, bashed gently with a rolling pin or other suitable implement and cut into 4

30g fresh ginger, sliced

3 kaffir lime leaves, shredded

1 tsp dried chilli flakes

1 tbsp soy sauce

1 tbsp fish sauce (nam pla)

cooked, use a flat, heatproof rubber spatula to fold the omelette in half. Slide on to a plate and keep somewhere warm while you make the remaining omelettes.

To serve, garnish with coriander leaves and a spoonful of the sambal.

100g white sugar
15g Maldon salt or other
 flaky sea salt

For the omelettes:
12 eggs
3 tsp Smoked Chilli Sambal
 (see page 22), plus extra
 to serve
butter for frying
1 green chilli, sliced
 into super-fine rounds
a bunch of spring onions,
 sliced
leaves from a bunch
 of coriander

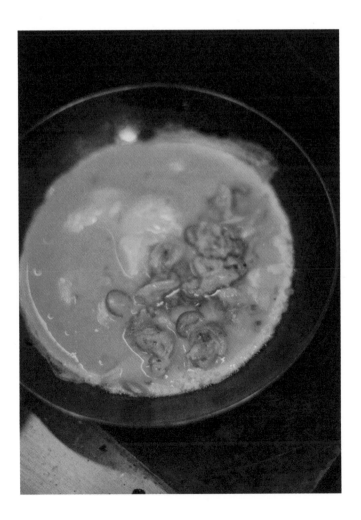

Tea-smoked Salmon and Coconut Fishcakes with Yuzu Hollandaise

If you cannot summon the will to smoke your own salmon or you are short of time, you can buy perfectly good smoked fish from your local fishmonger or supermarket. This recipe works just as well with smoked mackerel or haddock.

Salted yuzu juice is available from most Japanese grocery stores. If you cannot find it, serve the fishcakes with a lemon hollandaise made with the juice of a lemon. I also like to serve them with spinach wilted with lemon juice and/or a poached egg.

First smoke the salmon. Mix together the sugar, salt and oil. Smother the flesh of the salmon with it and leave in the fridge for 20–40 minutes.

Line a wok or a heavy-based roasting tin with foil and tip in the rice and tea leaves, mixing them together. Place a wire cake rack on top of this.

Remove the salmon from the fridge and scrape most of the sugar and salt mix off the flesh. Place the fish skin-side down on the rack and cover the entire rack with a loose tent of foil, making sure that there is room for the smoke to circulate freely.

Place the wok or roasting tin on the hob over a high heat until it begins to smoke (you'll be able to smell it). Turn the heat down a little (it should be moderately high) and leave to smoke for 8 minutes, then check its progress. The salmon should be pink and translucent and not quite cooked through.

Remove from the heat and leave to cool. Remove the skin, scrape off the brown bloodline, then break the salmon up into large flakes.

Cook the potatoes in boiling salted water until tender, then drain well and mash with the butter and some salt and pepper. Add the coconut powder, spring onions, coriander and lemon zest and mix gently but thoroughly. Add the smoked salmon and mix again, being careful not to break up the salmon flakes too much. Cool the mixture and refrigerate until ready to cook. You can do this up to 24 hours in advance.

Serves 6
600g floury potatoes,
    peeled and cut into chunks
100g unsalted butter, melted,
    plus extra for frying
150g coconut powder
    (or 100g desiccated
    coconut)
5 spring onions, finely
    chopped
a bunch of coriander, chopped
grated zest of 1 lemon
polenta and desiccated
    coconut for coating
Maldon salt or other
    flaky sea salt
black pepper

For the tea-smoked salmon:
50g soft brown sugar or
    demerara sugar
20g Maldon salt or other
    flaky sea salt
50ml sesame oil
400g piece of salmon
    fillet, skin on
150g white rice
(any sort will do)
50g loose tea leaves
    (builder's tea is fine –
    but you could use

Divide the mixture into 6 or 12 and shape into cakes. Coat in a mixture of half polenta and half desiccated coconut. Heat a little butter in a heavy-based frying pan and fry the fishcakes in batches until golden brown on both sides. Place them on a parchment-lined baking tray and bake in an oven preheated to 180°C/Gas Mark 4 for 20 minutes, until cooked through.

Meanwhile, make the hollandaise. Gently melt the butter in a pan and keep warm. In a heatproof glass bowl, whisk together the egg yolks, whole egg, yuzu and lemon juice. Place the bowl over a pan of gently simmering water, making sure the water doesn't touch the base of the bowl, and whisk continuously until it begins to thicken. Remove from the heat and, still whisking constantly, pour in the warm melted butter a little at a time – as if you were making mayonnaise. Once all the butter has been incorporated, check the seasoning. Cover with cling film and put aside in a warm place until ready to use.

To serve, divide the fishcakes between six plates and spoon over a generous helping of the hollandaise.

jasmine for a more
delicate flavour)

For the yuzu hollandaise:
250g unsalted butter
3 egg yolks
1 egg
60ml salted yuzu juice
a squeeze of lemon juice

Turkish Menemen with Sumac Yoghurt

I was taught this exceptionally simple yet knockout brunch dish by a Kiwi–Turkish couple, Claire and Zeki, at whose restaurant in Auckland, New Zealand, I held my first head-chef position. What a brilliant year that was, not least because it was where I first discovered Turkish chilli flakes in all their glory, my favourite of all chillies!

We served a version of this in individual pans, which is always impressive if you have enough to go around. Make sure you wrap a cloth napkin around the handles, though, to avoid lawsuits.

First make the sumac yoghurt: whisk the olive oil into the yoghurt along with the sumac, garlic and lemon juice, adding more of the latter if you like. Season to taste with salt and pepper and set aside.

Heat the olive oil in a large, heavy-bottomed frying pan, add the fennel, cumin and mustard seeds and the Aleppo chilli flakes and sauté for 4–5 minutes, until the spices are aromatic. Add the ginger, onion and garlic and cook until softened, then add the red pepper and tomatoes. Cook gently for 10 minutes or so, until the sauce is aromatic and beginning to thicken. Check the seasoning, then crack the eggs on top and leave the sauce to simmer gently away beneath for about 5 minutes, until the eggs are cooked to your liking. Remove from the heat, sprinkle with extra virgin olive oil and plenty of chopped parsley and serve from the pan, accompanied by the sumac yoghurt.

Serves 4
2 tbsp olive oil
2 tsp fennel seeds
1 tsp cumin seeds
¼ tsp mustard seeds
1 tsp Aleppo chilli flakes
a knob of fresh ginger, grated
1 red onion, finely diced
2 garlic cloves, finely chopped
1 red pepper, diced
6 vine-ripened tomatoes, diced (or a 400g can of tomatoes will do)
4 eggs, preferably organic or free range
extra virgin olive oil, to serve
a bunch of flat-leaf parsley, chopped

For the sumac yoghurt:
50ml extra virgin olive oil
200g natural or Greek yoghurt
1 tbsp sumac
½ tsp crushed garlic
a squeeze of lemon juice
Maldon salt or other flaky sea salt
black pepper

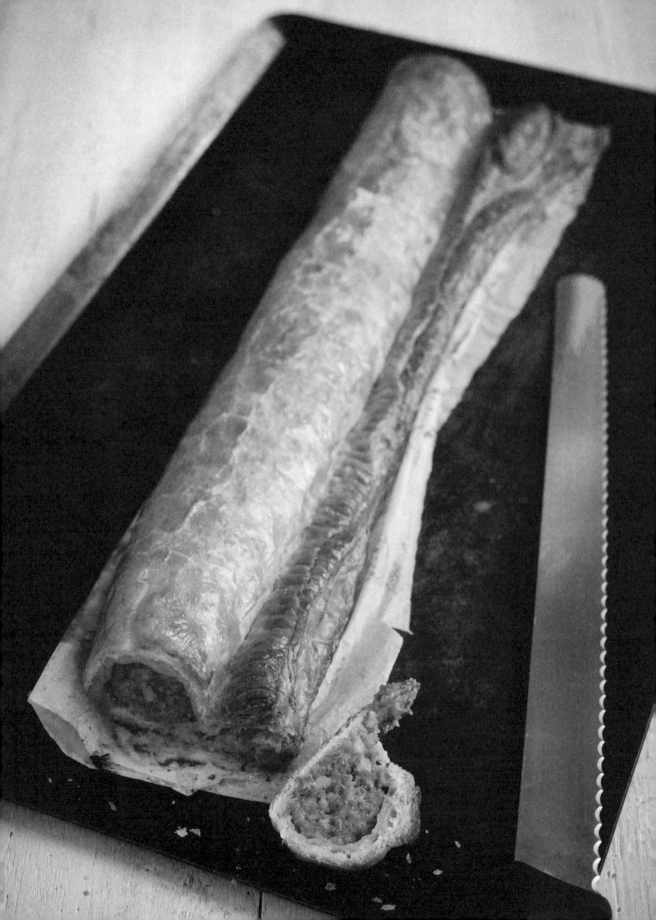

THE MODERN PANTRY SAUSAGE ROLLS

Sausage rolls are one of my guilty pleasures. What could possibly be better than light, flaky, buttery pastry filled with moist, unctuous porky goodness? This is the recipe we make at The Modern Pantry. It has a hint of smokiness reminiscent of chorizo, another of my favourites.

Sausage rolls can be made well in advance and frozen. Bake from frozen at the same temperature, giving them an extra 5–10 minutes.

Cook the onion in the oil over a moderate heat until tender and caramelised. Tip into a bowl large enough to hold all the remaining ingredients and leave to cool completely. Add the minced meat and back fat, plus the breadcrumbs, salt, pepper, smoked paprika and thyme, and mix thoroughly. Check the mix for seasoning by frying a small piece in a pan and tasting, adding a little more salt if necessary.

Divide the mixture in half and shape into two 30cm logs. Place each log on a sheet of puff pastry and brush some of the beaten egg along one pastry edge. Fold the pastry over and seal it as carefully as possible, pressing down firmly with the back of a fork along the flat edge.

Cut each log into six rolls, place on a baking sheet and brush with the remaining beaten egg. Bake in an oven preheated to 200°C/Gas Mark 6 for 20–25 minutes, until golden and cooked through. Serve hot or at room temperature, with Tomato Relish (see page 37) or, dare I say, tomato ketchup!

MAKES 12

1 large onion, finely
  sliced into half moons
1 tbsp vegetable oil
300g pork belly, minced
300g pork shoulder, minced
50g pork back fat, minced
35g breadcrumbs
2 tsp salt
¼ tsp black pepper
1 tsp sweet smoked paprika
1 tsp chopped thyme
2 sheets of puff pastry,
  30cm x 15cm each
1 egg, lightly beaten

SNACKS AND SMALL PLATES

LEMON AND CARAWAY BRAISED RAINBOW CHARD WITH GARLIC BRUSCHETTA

Using a sharp paring knife, separate the chard stalks from the leaves. Bring a large pan of water to a rapid boil, add a little salt and blanch the stalks for a minute or two, then drain and refresh them in a bowl of iced water. Drain the stalks again and cut them into 1cm lengths. Roughly shred the chard leaves but keep them separate from the stalks.

In a pan large enough to hold the chard, warm the olive oil over a moderate heat. Add the lemon zest and leave to bubble for 1 minute, then add the sliced garlic, chilli, rosemary and caraway seeds. When the garlic begins to caramelise, add the chard stalks, lemon juice and a decent pinch of salt. Cover with a lid, reduce the heat and leave to simmer for 3–4 minutes, until the stalks are tender. Add the leaves and continue to cook until they too are tender. Check the seasoning, adding more lemon juice, if you like, as well as some salt and pepper.

To serve, grill the sourdough bread and rub with the remaining garlic clove. Don't worry about peeling it; the juices will break through and do their job. Spoon the braised chard and its juices over the bruschetta, as well as a little extra virgin olive oil, and eat immediately.

SERVES 6

1 bunch of rainbow chard (or Swiss chard if you can't find any), about 500g
150ml olive oil
zest of 1 lemon, removed with a potato peeler and roughly chopped
4 garlic cloves, 3 finely sliced and 1 left whole
1 red chilli, split lengthways
2 sprigs of rosemary, chopped
1 tsp caraway seeds
juice of ½ lemon
6 slices of sourdough bread
Maldon salt or other flaky sea salt
black pepper
extra virgin olive oil, to serve

GRILLED HALLOUMI AND LEMON ROAST FENNEL BRUSCHETTA WITH CRISPY CAPERS

Cut the halloumi into six even slices across its width. Leave to soak in cold water for at least 2 hours, preferably overnight. This helps reduce the saltiness of the cheese and also yields a softer, more mozzarella-like texture when cooked.

Trim the fennel bulbs and cut each one into six lengthways. Put in a bowl. Peel the lemons with a potato peeler. Remove excess white pith from the zest using a sharp paring knife and then cut into very fine strips. Juice the lemons and add to the fennel, along with the strips of lemon zest, fennel seeds and olive oil. Season with salt and pepper and toss together well. Tip the mixture out on to a parchment-lined baking sheet, cover with foil and bake in an oven preheated to 180°C/Gas Mark 4 for 20 minutes or until the fennel is almost tender. Remove the foil and cook for a further 10–15 minutes, until the fennel has begun to caramelise and turn golden. Remove from the oven and leave to cool.

Pat the capers dry on a piece of kitchen paper. Heat 100ml of the vegetable oil in a frying pan, add the capers and cook for 2–3 minutes, until they are crisp. Remove with a slotted spoon and leave to drain on kitchen paper.

Heat the remaining vegetable oil over a moderate heat in a pan large enough to hold the halloumi comfortably. Thoroughly pat dry the halloumi slices and, when the pan is hot, carefully place them in it. Cook over a moderate heat until golden brown underneath, then turn over and cook until the other side is golden.

Meanwhile, grill the sourdough, then rub one side with the clove of garlic. Don't worry about peeling it. Once you start rubbing it on the toast, the juices will break through and do their job. Place a piece of toast on each plate. Toss the fennel with the watercress and pile on to the toast. Lay a slice of halloumi on each, then scatter over the crispy capers. Drizzle a little extra virgin olive oil over and serve with a wedge of lemon.

SERVES 6
1 250g block of
    halloumi cheese
4 fennel bulbs
2 lemons, plus lemon
    wedges to serve
2 tsp fennel seeds
125ml extra virgin olive oil,
    plus extra to serve
3 tbsp baby capers
130ml vegetable oil
6 slices of sourdough bread
1 garlic clove
leaves from a bunch
    of watercress
Maldon salt or other
    flaky sea salt
black pepper

GLOBE ARTICHOKE, RED ONION, TARRAGON AND PARMESAN CROSTINI

One of my hero flavours is anise, whether it comes from star anise, fennel, liquorice or any other ingredient with a similar flavour profile. Tarragon and artichoke are two such ingredients. Their anise notes complement each other perfectly and make for a fabulous flavour sensation. If globe artichokes are out of season use roasted Jerusalem artichokes. Instead of using this as a crostini topping, you could serve it as a salad. Rather than finely chopping everything up just toss the ingredients together with some rocket or watercress and serve with the Parmesan shavings on top.

Those of you who are lucky enough to have a garden , if you happen to have any baby nasturtium flowers to hand, scatter the flowers or leaves over the crostini and be sure to eat them. Speaking of which, you can also toss a few small nasturtium leaves though a mixed green salad to add an interesting dimension.

Cut the baguette into slices 3mm thick, lay them on a baking sheet and sprinkle with olive oil and the salt and pepper. Place in an oven preheated to 140°C/Gas Mark 1 and bake for about 20 minutes, until golden and crisp. Leave to cool.

Heat the 2 tablespoons of oil over a moderate heat and add the fennel seeds. Fry for a moment or two, until aromatic, then add the onion and garlic. Fry, stirring from time to time, until the onion is completely soft and caramelised. Remove from the heat and leave to cool.

Put the chopped artichoke hearts in a bowl and stir in the onion mixture, tarragon, grated Parmesan and lemon juice. Spread liberally over the crostini, shave over a little extra Parmesan and serve immediately.

SERVES 6

1 day-old thin baguette
2 tbsp olive oil, plus
   extra for sprinkling
¼ tsp Maldon salt or
   other flaky sea salt
¼ tsp black pepper
1 tsp fennel seeds
1 red onion, finely sliced
   into half moons
1 garlic clove, chopped
2 large Confit Artichoke
   Hearts (see page 128),
   finely chopped
2 tsp chopped tarragon
1½ tbsp finely grated
Parmesan cheese, plus
   a block of Parmesan
   for shaving
a squeeze of lemon juice

TRUFFLED BEETROOT, BASIL AND MASCARPONE CROSTINI

Finely slice the beetroot, preferably on a mandoline. Place in a roasting tin, add the vinegar, olive oil, pomegranate molasses, basil stalks, lemongrass and ¼ teaspoon of salt and mix thoroughly. Cover with foil and bake in an oven preheated to 180°C/Gas Mark 4 for 25 minutes, until the beetroot is tender but still has a bit of crunch. Remove from the oven and check the seasoning and acidity, adding a little more salt or vinegar if required. Leave to cool.

Remove the basil stalks and lemongrass from the beetroot. Shred the basil leaves and add to the beetroot with the truffle oil, stirring them in thoroughly. You may add more truffle oil if you like. I prefer the subtle approach.

Cut the baguette into slices 3mm thick and lay them on a baking sheet. Sprinkle with olive oil, salt and pepper and bake in an oven preheated to 140°C/Gas Mark 1 for about 20 minutes, until golden and crisp. Leave to cool, then lightly rub each piece with the garlic cloves.

To serve, spread a generous layer of mascarpone on to each crostini and pile on the beetroot.

SERVES 4

350g raw beetroot, peeled
4 tbsp Chardonnay vinegar
3 tbsp extra virgin olive oil, plus extra for sprinkling
4tsp pomegranate molasses
4 basil sprigs, leaves picked, leaves and stalks reserved
1 lemongrass stalk, trimmed, bashed and chopped
1 tsp best-quality white truffle oil
1 day-old thin baguette (or other stale bread)
2 garlic cloves
250g mascarpone cheese
Maldon salt or other flaky sea salt
black pepper

BAKED RICOTTA AND BEE POLLEN CAKES WITH MANUKA HONEY AND LEMON DRESSING

Lucques olives are a perfect accompaniment to this dish but any fruity green olive will do; maybe a shard of lavosh (see page 218), too.

For more information about using bee pollen and where to source it see page 235.

Mix the ricotta, Parmesan, lemon zest, thyme and bee pollen together in a bowl and season to taste.

Line a baking sheet with baking parchment, put four 6cm metal rings on top and divide the ricotta mix between them. Grate extra Parmesan on top and sprinkle with bee pollen. If you are feeling racy, sprinkle a little dried chilli on top too. Bake in an oven preheated to 180°C/Gas Mark 4 for 8–10 minutes, until golden. Remove from the oven and leave to cool.

Whisk all the ingredients for the dressing together and toss with the salad leaves, adding just enough to coat them lightly. Serve the cakes with the dressed salad leaves and green olives.

SERVES 4
500g ricotta cheese
50g Parmesan cheese,
    freshly grated, plus
    extra for sprinkling
2 tsp grated lemon zest
1 tsp chopped thyme
3 tsp bee pollen, plus
    extra for sprinkling
a little dried chilli (optional)
a scattering of bitter salad
    leaves, such as chicory
a few green olives
Maldon salt or other
    flaky sea salt
black pepper

For the dressing:
1 tbsp Manuka honey
juice of 1 lemon
zest of ½ lemon
75ml extra virgin olive oil
¼ tsp Maldon salt or other
flaky sea salt
black pepper

HIJIKI, SOY AND SESAME RICE CRACKERS

Cook the rice in the water over a low heat until it is completely soft and has the consistency of porridge. Add all the remaining ingredients except the oil and mix thoroughly. Spread the mixture evenly on to non-stick baking mats or baking parchment and top with another sheet of baking parchment. Using a rolling pin, flatten the mixture further to a layer about 5mm thick then gently lift off the top sheet of baking parchment. Leave to dry somewhere warm overnight. Alternatively, you can speed up the process by drying the mixture in the oven at 100°C for an hour or so. It is important that the rice is completely dry or the crackers won't puff up when you fry them.

Heat a 10cm depth of oil in a heavy-based pan over a moderate heat. Break the rice into cracker-sized shards and fry, flipping them halfway through cooking to ensure they are crisp on both sides. This will only take a couple of minutes. Test one on its own to start with, to get an idea of how much they will puff up and therefore how many you can cook at once.

Drain on kitchen paper and season with a little more salt if required. Cool and store in an airtight container for up to one week until ready to eat. Serve with a selection of pickles or relishes, as you would poppadoms, or alongside a curry or simply on their own.

500g glutinous rice
    or risotto rice
1.5 litres water
1 tsp Maldon salt or
    other flaky sea salt
2 tbsp Soy-braised Hijiki
    (see page 43)
2 tsp light soy sauce
1¼ tbsp sesame seeds
rapeseed oil for frying

GRILLED AUBERGINE WITH YUZU SOY DRESSING

Make the dressing by whisking all the ingredients together in a bowl. Set aside until ready to use.

Prick each aubergine several times with a fork, brush with a little vegetable oil, then bake in an oven preheated to 200°C/ Gas Mark 6 for 20 minutes or until just tender. They should have collapsed slightly but still hold their shape. Don't worry if they have totally collapsed, you can still use them! If you have a barbecue or a ridged grill pan, you could cook the aubergines on this, rolling them over from time to time to ensure even cooking. This will impart a deliciously smoky flavour to them.

When the aubergines are cool enough to handle, peel them carefully so as to keep them intact, then place on a dish. Spoon over the dressing, pile on the crispy shallots and scatter with the Thai basil. Serve immediately.

SERVES 3
3 small aubergines
a little vegetable oil
Crispy Shallots (see page 25)
30 Thai basil leaves
   (or coriander leaves if you
   cannot find Thai basil)

For the yuzu soy dressing:
50ml soy sauce
70ml mirin
35ml salted yuzu juice
2 tbsp water
1 tbsp sesame oil
a small thumb-sized piece of
   fresh ginger, finely chopped
½ red chilli, finely chopped

FETA, DATE AND SWEETCORN FRITTERS

This is a wonderful example of how ingredients from different cultures can be combined to great effect. Here the fresh turmeric, curry leaves and sweet dates add a distinctly Indian fragrance and are balanced perfectly with the saltiness of the Greek feta. East meets West in a fritter.

Heat the olive oil over a high heat in a heavy-bottomed pan until smoking, then add the curry leaves, fennel and cumin seeds, turmeric and chilli. Fry until aromatic, reduce the heat slightly, then add the red onions and cook for 10–15 minutes, until caramelised. Remove from the heat, tip into a bowl and leave to cool. Add the feta, dates, sweetcorn, spring onions, coriander and parsley.

Sift all the dry ingredients into a large bowl. Whisk the buttermilk and eggs together and stir into the dry ingredients, mixing thoroughly. Add the feta and date mixture and stir well to combine.

Heat some rapeseed oil in a deep-fat fryer or a large, deep pan. Drop dessertspoonfuls of the batter into the hot oil and fry until golden, flipping the fritters over in the oil to ensure even cooking. Remove with a slotted spoon, drain on kitchen paper and leave in a warm spot while you cook the rest.

Serve immediately, with Tomato Relish and some Greek yoghurt, if you like.

SERVES AT LEAST 8
2 tbsp olive oil
10 curry leaves, chopped
2 tsp fennel seeds
2 tsp cumin seeds
2 tsp finely grated fresh
    turmeric (or 1 tsp
    ground turmeric)
½ green chilli, finely chopped
400g red onions, sliced finely
    into half moons
200g feta cheese,
    cut into 5mm dice
200g dates, cut into 5mm dice
kernels from 2 corn cobs
    or 300g tinned
    sweetcorn, drained
5 spring onions, finely
    sliced into rounds
a large bunch of coriander,
    chopped
a large bunch of flat-leaf
    parsley, chopped
170g besan flour (also known
    as gram or chickpea flour)
75g polenta
½ tsp bicarbonate of soda
¾ tsp baking powder
½ tsp table salt
150ml buttermilk
2 eggs
rapeseed oil for deep-frying

To serve:
Tomato Relish (see page 37)
Greek yoghurt (optional)

CRAB RAREBIT

My fabulous sous-chef Robert Mcleary and I developed this take on a classic Welsh rarebit as a tribute to Fergus Henderson, whose rarebit is legendary. Although one would not normally pair crab with Cheddar the rich, creamy brown crab meat stands up to the challenge brilliantly. Make sure you don't skimp on the white crab meat to pile on top.

Melt the butter in a pan over a moderate heat. When it begins to bubble, stir in the flour and continue to cook for a minute or so, until it smells biscuity. Reduce the heat and gradually stir in the milk. Continue to stir until the mixture comes to the boil and becomes thick and paste-like. Remove from the heat and add the egg yolks, Worcestershire sauce, mustard, Cheddar and brown crab meat. Transfer to a bowl and leave to cool completely. Whisk the egg whites to stiff peaks and gently fold them into the cooled mixture in three lots. Refrigerate until ready to serve. This can be done a day in advance.

To serve, toast the slices of bread, then generously slather with the rarebit, being careful to cover the toast completely or the edges will burn. Place under a hot grill and cook until the rarebit bubbles and is golden. Transfer to serving plates, scatter with the white crab meat and a dusting of chilli flakes, plus a drizzle of Prawn Oil (see page 40), should you have any in your fridge. Serve immediately, with the lime wedges.

SERVES 6

30g unsalted butter
30g plain flour
160ml milk
3 eggs, separated
1½ tbsp Worcestershire sauce
1½ tbsp English mustard
75g tasty Cheddar cheese, grated
250g brown crab meat
6 slices of crusty white bread or sourdough
100g white crab meat
shichimi flakes or Urfa chill flakes, for dusting
a little Prawn Oil (see page 40), if you like
1 lime, cut into wedges

SMOKED HADDOCK FINGERS
WITH SEAWEED TARTARE SAUCE

This is our version of (wheat-free) fish fingers, delicious served with
seaweed tartare sauce or even a mustard mayo. Some spinach wilted
in a knob of butter with a squeeze of lemon juice makes a perfect side.

Put the smoked haddock in a pan, pour over the milk and bring
to a gentle simmer. Cover and simmer until just cooked; this will
only take a few minutes. Leave to cool. Transfer the haddock to
a plate and gently flake the flesh, discarding the skin and any
bones. Strain the poaching liquor into a large measuring jug,
pour in any additional juices the haddock has released, then
top up with enough water to bring the total volume of liquid
to 1.2 litres. Put the besan flour, salt and pepper in a bowl and
slowly add the liquid, whisking well to prevent lumps.

Heat the vegetable oil over a moderate heat in a heavy-bottomed
pan large enough to hold the besan batter. Add the fennel
seeds and fry for a minute or so, until aromatic. Add the spring
onions, parsley and lemon zest and cook for a further minute
or two, then add the besan batter. Stir continuously until the
mixture is thick and comes away from the sides of the pan;
this will probably take about 10 minutes. If it gets lumpy, use
a whisk to beat it into submission. Add the smoked haddock
flakes and continue to cook, stirring all the while, for a further
3–4 minutes.

Use a spatula to scrape the mixture out into an oiled 20 x 15cm
deep-sided tin dusted with polenta. Quickly wet your hands in
a bowl of cold water and flatten the batter out evenly, dipping
your hands in the water as needed. Sprinkle a little more
polenta on top, press it in and leave to cool. Chill until firm.

Meanwhile, make the tartare sauce: place the yolks, mustard
and lemon juice in a food processor and turn on, then pour in
the oils in a slow, thin stream. If making by hand, put the yolks,
mustard and lemon juice in a bowl and whisk together. Again,
pour in the oils in a slow, thin stream, whisking all the while.
It is essential that you do not rush this or your mayonnaise
will split. If this does happen, however, don't panic! Just start
again with 1 egg yolk this time, slowly whisk/blend in the
split mixture and it will come back together.

SERVES 6
400g smoked haddock
300ml milk
400g besan flour (also known
    as gram or chickpea flour)
½ tsp salt
½ tsp black pepper
1 tbsp vegetable oil
2 tsp fennel seeds
5 spring onions, finely sliced
a bunch of flat-leaf parsley,
    chopped
grated zest of 1 lemon
polenta for dusting
rapeseed oil for deep-frying

For the seaweed
tartare sauce:
2 egg yolks
1 tbsp Dijon mustard
juice of ½ lemon
300ml vegetable oil or
    light olive oil
100ml extra virgin olive oil
80g Soy-braised Hijiki
    (see page 43)
30g baby capers
½ bunch of flat-leaf parsley,
    finely chopped
Maldon salt or other
    flaky sea salt
black pepper

Transfer the mayonnaise from the food processor to a bowl, add the remaining ingredients and mix well. Check the seasoning, adding salt and more lemon juice if required.

Heat some rapeseed oil to 180° in a deep-fat fryer or a large, deep pan. Cut the chilled fish mixture into chunky fingers, gently roll them in a little more polenta, then fry in batches until crisp and golden. If you prefer, you can shallow-fry the fish fingers in a little oil over a medium heat for 3–4 minutes on each side. Drain on kitchen paper and serve immediately with the sauce.

SASHIMI

Sashimi is one of those simple yet knockout dishes we rarely think to serve at home. It makes a perfect snack on a hot summer's day or a starter for any meal. The key is super-fresh fish, so make sure that is what you buy when visiting your fishmonger.

Here are three of my favourite sashimi recipes. You can make all the dressings in advance, though not more than a day, and you must feel free to replace my fish suggestions with whatever is best at the time. Sea bass, snapper and sea trout all make good substitutes.

KINGFISH SASHIMI WITH KALAMANSI LIME, GREEN TEA AND WASABI DRESSING

Slice the kingfish fillet lengthwise down the middle, following the natural line. Turn the pieces of fillet over and, using a sharp knife, carefully trim away the blood line – the brownish seam that runs the length of the fillet. Turn the fillet over again and cut into 5mm strips, or thicker if you prefer, crossways this time. Divide the sashimi between six small plates.

Whisk the lime juice, kalamansi lime juice, mirin, soy, green tea and wasabi paste together. Dress the fish liberally with this mixture.

Remove the stalks from the sorrel and slice finely. Scatter the sorrel over the fish.

If you have found some tomatillos and/or wasabi tobiko, remove the papery husk of the tomatillos and dice finely. Mix with the wasabi tobiko and sprinkle this over the sashimi too. Scatter over the celery cress, if using, and serve immediately.

SERVES 6

500g skinned kingfish fillet, preferably the fleshy end of the fillet as opposed to the tail
50ml lime juice
50ml kalamansi lime juice
50ml mirin
40ml light soy sauce
1 tsp mancha green tea
1 tsp wasabi paste
a bunch of sorrel
2 tomatillos (optional)
1 tbsp wasabi tobiko (optional)
celery cress, to garnish (optional)

ORGANIC SALMON SASHIMI WITH UMEBOSHI PLUM AND YUZU DRESSING

Prepare the salmon fillet according to the instructions in the kingfish sashimi recipe opposite.

Whisk the yuzu juice, lime juice, mirin, vegetable oil and umeboshi together. Check for seasoning and acidity, adding a little salt or more lime juice if needed. Dress the sashimi liberally with the mixture and serve immediately.

SERVES 6
500g skinned organic salmon
   fillet, preferably the fleshy
   end of the fillet as opposed
   to the tail
50ml salted yuzu juice
50ml lime juice
40ml mirin
1 tbsp vegetable oil
3 umeboshi plums, stoned
   and finely chopped
Maldon salt or other
   flaky sea salt

SCALLOP SASHIMI WITH TRUFFLED BLACK MUSTARD SEED AND SOY DRESSING

If you can't get your hands on any good quality truffle oil or you are not a fan, this recipe is still perfect without.

Clean each scallop by removing the hard white muscle from its side, along with the poo sac and the roe. Carefully slice the scallops horizontally so that you end up with beautiful white rounds – three or four slices per scallop, depending on how thick and plump they are.

Heat a small frying pan over a moderate heat and add the mustard seeds. Toast gently until they begin to pop and are aromatic. Whisk together the soy, yuzu, lime juice, water and mirin, then add the mustard seeds. Lastly whisk in the truffle oil.

Divide the scallops between six small plates and pour over the dressing, but don't overdo it in this instance. It is easy to overwhelm the delicate sweetness of the scallops. You can always add more. Scatter over the sorrel, if using, and serve immediately.

SERVES 6
12 medium or 6 large,
   very fresh king scallops
1 rounded tsp black
   mustard seeds
50ml light soy sauce
2 tbsp salted yuzu juice
40ml lime juice
40ml water
2 tbsp mirin
3 tsp best-quality
   white truffle oil
buckler leaf sorrel,
   to garnish (optional)

GARLICKY SNAILS WITH CHORIZO MASH

Chorizo mash has to be one of my favourite mashes ever. The Urfa chilli flakes add an earthy richness, but if you don't have any it will be just as delicious without.

You could serve this mash with almost anything. Slow-roast pork belly (see page 172) or a nice, chunky piece of cod are two good choices, but it is particularly good served as a small plate with garlicky snails. Although it is possible to buy fresh snails in the UK, purchasing good-quality tinned snails is perfectly acceptable and definitely easier – any decent deli should stock them.

First make the chorizo mash. Cook the potatoes in boiling salted water until tender, drain thoroughly and then mash.

While the potatoes are cooking, peel the skin off the chorizo and cut the meat into small pieces, then, using the flat of your knife, mash it roughly. Put the chorizo in a small pan and fry over a low heat until the fat has melted and the chorizo is cooked. Add the cream and Urfa flakes, bring to the boil and stir into the mash. Taste and season if necessary. If the potatoes seem a little dry, add more cream.

Drain and rinse the snails, reserving a couple of tablespoons of the juice from the can. Melt the 2 tablespoons of butter in a frying pan over a moderately high heat and, when bubbling and beginning to brown, add the garlic. Sauté for 20 seconds or so, then add the snails and continue to cook for a minute, shaking the pan to prevent the garlic overbrowning. Add the red wine, chicken stock and reserved snail juices, plus a pinch of salt, then reduce the heat to a rapid simmer and cook for 3–4 minutes, until the gravy begins to thicken. Add the parsley and the knob of butter and check the seasoning.

Put a generous spoonful of mash and six snails into each of eight small bowls, spoon over the pan juices and scatter with the shallots and sorrel. Serve immediately.

SERVES AT LEAST 8
48 canned snails
2 tbsp unsalted butter,
    plus a knob
3 garlic cloves,
    finely chopped
80ml red wine
100ml chicken stock,
    preferably dark
    (see page 39)
½ bunch of flat-leaf
    parsley, chopped
Crispy Shallots (see page 25)
1 bunch of sorrel, shredded
Maldon salt or other
    flaky sea salt

For the chorizo mash:
1kg floury potatoes, peeled
250g spicy cooking chorizo
100ml double cream, plus
    a bit more if needed
¾ tsp Urfa chilli flakes

PIGS' CHEEKS BRAISED WITH CIDER, FENNEL AND BAY

You may have gathered by the number of pork related dishes that appear in this book that I am a fan. Hands down it is my favourite meat both to cook and eat, every inch of it begging to be transformed into some delicious morsel or other. Pig cheeks are no exception. They have a rich, gelatinous texture, which is not dissimilar to that of beef shin, and an irresistible porky flavour.

Serve with Crispy Shallots (see page 25), parsley and a chunk of crusty bread or Cumin-roast Parsnip and Plantain Mash (see page 137).

Blend the salt, sugar, spices, ginger, garlic and bay leaves to a fine paste in a food processor, then coat the pigs' cheeks in this mixture and leave to marinate overnight.

The next day, lightly rinse the cheeks (leaving on some of the marinade is good), put them in an ovenproof dish just large enough to hold them and add all the remaining ingredients. Cover with a lid or foil and braise in an oven preheated to 140°C/Gas Mark 1 for approximately 1 hour, until the cheeks are soft and gelatinous.

SERVES 8

800g pigs' cheeks, trimmed
   of sinew and excess fat
4 shallots, chopped
200ml cider
200ml white wine
200ml Dark Chicken Stock
   (see page 39) or ordinary
   chicken stock

For the marinade:
20g Maldon salt or
   other flaky sea salt
20g dark muscovado sugar
½ tsp juniper berries
½ tsp allspice
1 tsp fennel seeds
1 tsp Aleppo chilli flakes
30g fresh ginger
30g garlic cloves
4 large bay leaves

THIT HEO KHO

I came across this porkilicious delight at my local Vietnamese restaurant, Viet Garden, in Islington. Its sweet yet savoury unctuousness is delightful, and the pickles and salted duck egg that come with it there make for a perfectly balanced feast.

This is my interpretation, which we serve at The Modern Pantry as a small plate with pickled beansprouts and lotus root, crispy shallots and chopped coriander and spring onions. You can serve it with rice or mash or roast vegetables, if you like, and if you can't be bothered to make the pickles or crispy shallots, go and buy some! Try pickled walnuts for a not very authentic but pretty tasty alternative.

You can buy salted duck eggs in Asian supermarkets and if you have never tried them before, this is the dish to have them with. Put the eggs into cold water, bring up to the boil and cook for 6 minutes, then cut in half lengthways and serve in the shell. I like to scoop out the egg and mash it into the gravy.

Heat a little vegetable oil in a large, heavy-based frying pan and brown the diced pork in batches. Be careful not to overcrowd the pan or you will end up stewing the meat instead. When you have finished, deglaze the pan by pouring in the water and using a wooden spoon to scrape off all the caramelised goodness that has stuck to the base. Tip these juices into a casserole, then add the pork and all the remaining ingredients apart from those for serving, plus enough water to come halfway up the meat. The pork will create more juice as it cooks. Bring to a simmer, cover with a tight-fitting lid or foil and place in an oven preheated to 140°C/Gas Mark 1. Braise for an hour or so, until the meat is tender.

Serve simply, with all the accompaniments.

SERVES 4
a little vegetable oil
1kg pork neck or shoulder,
   cut into 2cm cubes
375ml water
4 shallots, chopped
4 garlic cloves, chopped
6 star anise
1 tbsp Chinese five-spice
   powder
125ml light soy sauce
100g palm sugar, grated
4 tbsp fish sauce (nam pla)

To serve:
leaves from a bunch
   of coriander
4 spring onions, sliced
Pickled Lotus Root
   (see page 28)
Crispy Shallots
   (see page 25)

KRUPUK QUAIL EGGS WITH CHILLI LIME DIPPING SAUCE

My dear friend Miles Kirby, Head Chef and co-owner of the fabulous Caravan restaurant in London, gave me the inspiration for these crisp golden globes of goodness one day while we were discussing the endless possibilities of the scotched egg. These are the kinds of conversation one has as a chef! You could make the krupuk crackers yourself but you can buy very good-quality ones in most Chinese supermarkets. If you can find the brand, Manora, labeled as Uncooked Shrimp Chips, which are made in Thailand, they are the best I have come across so far.

To cook the quail eggs, bring a pan of water to the boil, carefully put the eggs in and cook for 2½ minutes. Using a slotted spoon, quickly transfer the eggs to a bowl or colander and run them under cold water for 3–4 minutes to cool them down and thereby stop the cooking process. You want the eggs to be soft in the middle, so it is important that you get them out of the boiling water as soon as the time is up. Peel the eggs and set aside – don't worry if you have a few casualties.

To make the dipping sauce, cut the lime in half and squeeze out the juice. Put the juice and an empty lime half into a pan with all the remaining ingredients, bring to the boil and then simmer gently until syrupy. Remove from the heat and set aside.

Tip the krupuk crumbs into a medium bowl, put some flour into another and, in a third bowl, whisk the eggs. One by one, lightly dust the quail eggs in the flour, dip them into the whisked egg, then roll them in the crumbs. Once you have coated all the eggs, repeat the process. You may need another whisked egg and some extra crumbs. Refrigerate until ready to serve.

Heat some rapeseed oil in a deep-fat fryer or a large, deep pan and deep-fry the coated eggs for about a minute, until puffed and golden. Drain on kitchen paper and serve immediately, with the dipping sauce.

SERVES 6
24 quail eggs
500g raw krupuk crackers
    (see above), blitzed
    to coarse crumbs
plain flour for dusting
3–4 eggs
rapeseed oil for
    deep-frying

For the dipping sauce:
1 lime
300ml white wine
250ml water
150g palm sugar
1 red chilli,
    split lengthwise
3 star anise
2 pieces of asam
    (optional; if not using,
    add the juice of another
    lime)

CHORIZO SCOTCHED QUAIL EGGS

Quail eggs are perfect for small plates but you can use hen eggs too.
You'll need to cook hen eggs for slightly longer – 6 minutes rather than 4.

To cook the quail eggs, bring a pan of water to the boil, carefully put the eggs in and cook for 2½ minutes. Using a slotted spoon, quickly transfer the eggs to a bowl or colander and run them under cold water for 3–4 minutes to cool them down and thereby stop the cooking process. You want the eggs to be soft in the middle, so it is important that you get them out of the boiling water as soon as the time is up. Peel the eggs and set aside. If you thought 24 eggs seemed like a lot, you will by now see that it isn't, as you are bound to have a few casualties!

Next prepare the chorizo mixture. Heat the oil in a small pan until smoking, add the black onion and fennel seeds and the curry leaves and fry for a few seconds, until aromatic. Add the shallot and garlic, reduce the heat and sauté until soft. Remove from the heat and leave to cool.

Skin and roughly chop the chorizo, then mince it in a food processor. Put the chorizo, minced pork, spicy shallot mixture and salt into a bowl and mix thoroughly. Test the mixture for seasoning by frying a small patty in a pan, then add more salt to the remaining mixture if necessary. Chill thoroughly.

Flatten a tablespoon of the chorizo mixture into a disc in your palm. Place a quail egg in the centre, then bring the mix up to cover the egg, pressing the edges together to form a ball and making sure there are no holes in the mixture. Don't worry if the balls are not perfectly egg-shaped. Rustic is good! Once the eggs are wrapped, chill them for half an hour to firm up the meat. This will make them less fragile and easier to coat in the crumbs.

Tip the crumbs into a medium bowl, put some flour into another and, in a third bowl, whisk the eggs. One by one, lightly dust the wrapped quail eggs in the flour, dip them into the whisked egg, then roll in the crumbs. Once you have coated all the eggs, repeat the process. You may need another whisked egg and some extra crumbs. Refrigerate again for a further 30 minutes.

Heat the rapeseed oil in a deep-fat fryer or a large, deep pan and deep-fry the eggs for 3–4 minutes, until golden. Drain on kitchen paper. They can be served hot or cold, whole or cut in half.

SERVES 6–8
24 quail eggs
200g panko crumbs or
   plain breadcrumbs
plain flour for dusting
3 eggs
rapeseed oil for frying

For the chorizo mixture:
1 tbsp vegetable oil
1½ tsp black onion seeds
2 tsp fennel seeds
10 curry leaves,
   roughly chopped
1 shallot, finely diced
2 garlic cloves, finely chopped
200g spicy cooking chorizo
200g minced pork shoulder
½ tsp salt

SALADS

SPICED SALSIFY POACHED IN RED WINE, WITH PEARS, CASHEL BLUE AND TOASTED QUINOA

This recipe makes more toasted quinoa than you will need but any left over can be stored in an airtight container for up to two weeks. You can use it in salads, or as a garnish for roast pork or grilled fish to add crunch to them. Simply sprinkle over a tablespoon or two just before serving.

First prepare the toasted quinoa. Soak the quinoa in cold water for an hour.then drain in a sieve, rinse under cold water, shake well and leave to sit for 10 minutes. Heat a 1cm-deep layer of rapeseed oil in a pan over a moderate heat and fry the quinoa for about 5 minutes, stirring frequently, until golden and crisp. The oil should not be bubbling particularly frantically by this stage – another indication that the quinoa is ready, as the moisture has evaporated, meaning it will be crisp.

Drain the quinoa in a sieve set over a heatproof bowl, then tip it on to a tray lined with kitchen paper. Sprinkle over the five-spice powder and salt to taste, give it a good shake to make sure the seasoning is evenly blended, then leave to cool.

Scrub the salsify, peel off the brown, woody exterior and cut into 5cm lengths. Have to hand a bowl of cold water acidulated with lemon juice to drop the salsify into as you go; this will help to prevent it discolouring.

Put all the remaining salsify ingredients in a pan large enough to hold the salsify and bring to the boil. Reduce the heat to a gentle simmer, skim off any foam from the surface and leave to simmer for 10 minutes or so, until the poaching liquor is fragrant and syrupy.

Drain the salsify and add to the poaching liquor. Cook gently for 15–20 minutes, until tender, then remove from the heat and leave to cool in the syrup. You can bottle the salsify at this stage or store in an airtight container and refrigerate until ready to use. It will sit easily for a month or so in the fridge.

Layer the chard and chicory leaves with the salsify and pear in a large bowl or on individual plates. Crumble over the Cashel Blue, scatter with 3 tablespoons of the toasted quinoa and dress with a little of the salsify poaching liquor and some extra virgin olive oil. Serve immediately.

SERVES 6
100g baby chard leaves
2 heads of red chicory
2 ripe pears, each cut
  lengthways into 16 slices
200g Cashel Blue cheese
3 tbsp Toasted Quinoa
  (see below)
a little extra virgin olive oil

For the spiced salsify:
500g salsify
lemon juice
500ml red wine
150ml Cabernet
  Sauvignon vinegar
100g honey
1 red chilli,
  split lengthways
50g white sugar
3 star anise
4 cardamom seeds,
  lightly crushed
2 tsp fennel seeds

For the toasted quinoa:
80g quinoa
rapeseed oil for frying
1 tsp Chinese five-spice
  powder
table salt

QUINOA, TOMATILLO, PRESERVED LEMON AND MINT SALAD WITH SPICED TOASTED SEEDS

Super-healthy, tasty and bursting with fresh flavours, this salad is brilliant served alone or as an accompaniment to grilled meats or fish. Try it with the Chermoula-baked Sea Trout on page 149.

If you can't find tomatillo you can substitute green mango or Cape gooseberries.

First cook the seeds. Heat the oil in a heavy-bottomed frying pan over a moderate heat. Add the curry leaves and fry until aromatic, then add the fennel, caraway, nigella and mustard seeds. Reduce the heat a little and cook, shaking the pan, until the seeds begin to pop. Add the pumpkin and sunflower seeds. Keep shaking and tossing the seeds in the pan regularly to ensure even toasting. When they are golden, remove from the heat and add the salt and amchur. This will make more than you need for the salad but the seeds are super tasty and make a great snack.

For the salad, put the quinoa in a pan over a high heat and stir until lightly toasted. Add an equal volume of water, bring to the boil and simmer for about 5 minutes, until tender. Drain and set aside.

Heat the oil in a pan, add the onion and cook until tender and caramelised. Add the smoked paprika and sherry vinegar and continue to cook until the vinegar has evaporated. Toss with the quinoa, tomatillos, preserved lemon, mint, coriander, lime juice and a drizzle of extra virgin olive oil. Check the seasoning.

Arrange everything in layers in a bowl – first the mustard greens, then the quinoa, then a scattering of seeds. You should have two layers of each. Garnish with coriander leaves and serve immediately.

SERVES 6
250g quinoa
50ml olive oil
1 large red onion, sliced
¼ tsp sweet smoked paprika
50ml sherry vinegar
3 tomatillos, diced
1 tbsp finely diced preserved lemon (see page 34)
a handful of chopped mint
a handful of chopped coriander, plus a few extra leaves
juice of 1 lime
extra virgin olive oil for drizzling
100g mustard greens
Maldon salt or other flaky sea salt
black pepper

For the spiced toasted seeds:
2 tbsp olive oil
a handful of fresh curry leaves
2 tsp fennel seeds
2 tsp caraway seeds
1 tsp nigella (black onion) seeds
1 tsp black mustard seeds
200g pumpkin seeds
200g sunflower seeds
1 rounded tsp Maldon salt or other flaky sea salt
1 tbsp amchur

WILD RICE SALAD WITH CHARRED SWEETCORN, SPICED PECANS, AVOCADO AND MARINATED FETA

I love the earthy flavour and slightly chewy texture of wild rice, which is actually not a rice at all, it is a grain harvested from wild grass. Together with the smoky sweetness of the charred corn, the spicy crunch of the pecans, the creamy avocado and the salty punch of feta, this, to me, is a perfect salad.

Put the wild rice in a pan with the cinnamon stick and chilli, cover with plenty of water, then bring to the boil and simmer until the rice is tender but still al dente. Drain and leave to cool.

Meanwhile, prepare the charred sweetcorn. Slice the kernels off the cobs. Heat 1 tablespoon of the vegetable oil in a wok or large frying pan over a high heat until smoking. Add the corn and cook, shaking the pan from time to time, until it has a good colour. Remove from the heat and set aside. Heat the remaining oil in a pan, add the red onion and cook gently until soft and caramelised. Add the vinegar and smoked paprika and cook until the vinegar has evaporated. Remove from the heat, allow to cool and then add the sweetcorn and the salt.

Toss the pecans with the icing sugar, cumin seeds and a tablespoon of water. Spread them out on a baking tray and place in an oven preheated to 150°C/Gas Mark 2. Bake for 20 minutes or until golden, then remove from the oven and leave to cool.

Mix the rice with the sweetcorn and onion, then add the chopped coriander, avocado and watercress. Crumble over the feta and add the pecans.

SERVES 4
150g wild rice
1 small cinnamon stick
1 red chilli, split lengthways
a bunch of coriander, chopped
1 avocado, peeled, stoned
  and diced
a small bunch of watercress,
  tough stems removed
100g Marinated Feta
  (see page 27)

For the charred sweetcorn:
2 corn cobs
3 tbsp vegetable oil
1 red onion, sliced
3 tbsp good-quality
  red wine vinegar
¼ tsp sweet smoked paprika
½ tsp Maldon salt or other
  flaky sea salt

For the spiced pecans:
100g pecan nuts
1 tbsp icing sugar
1 tsp cumin seeds

BEETROOT, LENTIL AND MINT SALAD WITH POMEGRANATE MOLASSES AND ORANGE DRESSING

The beauty of this salad is its simplicity; its wonderful textures and flavours combining to create a refreshing yet earthy taste sensation. I have specified bull's blood salad leaves, so named for their beautiful colour, but watercress or rocket would also do. For a variation, try adding slices of fried halloumi and some Spiced Toasted Seeds (see page 106).

Heat the olive oil in a heavy-based pan, add the leek, onion and garlic and cook over a high heat until caramelised. Add the lentils, herbs and mirin and continue to fry for 4 minutes, stirring from time to time.

Pour over enough water to cover the lentils by 2–3cm, then bring to the boil and simmer for approximately 20 minutes, until the lentils are tender (if they begin to look dry, add a little more water). Remove from the heat and stir in the miso and soy sauce. Check the seasoning, adding more soy if needed, then leave to cool.

Whisk together all the ingredients for the dressing. Toss the beetroot, mint and lentils together in a bowl with a generous slosh of the dressing. Layer with the salad leaves and serve immediately.

SERVES 6

100ml extra virgin olive oil
1 small leek, cut in half lengthways and sliced
1 small red onion, sliced
4 garlic cloves, finely chopped
250g Puy lentils
1 tbsp each of chopped rosemary, thyme and sage
100ml mirin
40g white miso
50ml soy sauce
150g raw beetroot, peeled and cut into fine strips
a large handful of mint leaves, shredded
a couple of handfuls of bull's blood leaves

For the dressing:
1 tbsp pomegranate molasses
4 tbsp Cabernet Sauvignon vinegar
juice and grated zest of ½ orange
100ml extra virgin olive oil
a pinch of salt

CHERRY, OLIVE, BRAISED RED ONION AND COUSCOUS SALAD WITH TYMSBORO GOATS' CHEESE

Tymsboro is one of my favourite goats' cheeses. Its dense texture and delicate lemony flavour are perfect in this recipe alongside the fruity cherries and salty olives.

Put the sour cherries, apple juice and pomegranate molasses in a small pan and gently bring to the boil. Take off the heat and leave to cool. Strain the sour cherries, reserving the liquor, and chop them roughly, along with the olives.

Place the red onions in a parchment-lined roasting tin just large enough to hold them and pour over the vinegar and 80ml of the olive oil. Season, cover tightly with foil and bake in an oven preheated to 180°C/Gas Mark 4 for 25 minutes. Remove the foil, stir, then return to the oven for 10 minutes or so, until the onions are cooked through. Leave to cool.

Put the couscous in a large bowl and add the lemon juice and zest and enough cold water to cover by 1cm. Add the remaining olive oil and some salt and pepper and mix thoroughly. Cover with cling film and leave to soak for 20 minutes or so, until the couscous has absorbed the water and is soft. Remove the cling film and fluff up the couscous with a fork, then mix in the sour cherries and olives, plus the fresh cherries and chopped herbs. Taste for seasoning.

Scatter a layer of watercress over a large platter, then some couscous followed by braised red onions and Tymsboro wedges. Repeat the layers until you have used everything up, then drizzle over the reserved liquor from the sour cherries and a little extra virgin olive oil.

SERVES 4

80g dried sour cherries
250ml apple juice
2 tbsp pomegranate molasses
100g Kalamata olives, pitted
2 red onions, sliced into
    rounds 1cm thick
80ml sherry vinegar or
    red wine vinegar
180ml extra virgin olive oil,
    plus extra for drizzling
350g instant couscous
juice and grated zest of
    1 lemon
250g fresh cherries,
    pitted and halved
a bunch of chervil,
    finely chopped
½ bunch of flat-leaf parsley,
    finely chopped
½ bunch of tarragon,
    finely chopped
3 bunches of watercress,
    woody stalks removed
1 Tymsboro goats' cheese,
    cut into thin wedges
Maldon salt or other
    flaky sea salt
black pepper

GRILLED CHICORY, AUBERGINE AND DATE SALAD WITH COCONUT LABNEH

First make the coconut labneh, which has to be prepared a couple of days in advance. Thoroughly whisk the yoghurt, coconut milk, coconut powder and salt together. Line a small sieve or colander with a clean piece of muslin, a new J-cloth or something similar and place on top of a bowl. Tip the yoghurt mixture in, then bring the sides of the cloth up to cover it completely. Weight the mixture down using a plate with cans on top, then place in the fridge and leave to drain for 48 hours. The labneh is ready when it is firm enough to roll into balls.

Mix the sumac and chilli flakes together on a plate. Shape the labneh into balls and gently roll them in the spices to give a light coating.

Halve the aubergines lengthways, then cut each half into five or six long wedges. Toss with the extra virgin olive oil, season with salt and pepper, then spread out on a parchment-lined baking sheet. Place in an oven preheated to 180°C/Gas Mark 4 and bake for 15 minutes or so, until the aubergines are tender and beginning to colour. Remove from the oven and leave to cool.

Heat the 2 tablespoons of olive oil in a heavy-based pan over a moderate heat, add the curry leaves and mustard seeds and fry for a minute or so, until aromatic. Scrunch up the pandan leaves and add them to the pan with the shallots and ginger. Reduce the heat slightly and cook for 5–10 minutes, stirring from time to time, until the shallots have become golden and caramelised. Add the dates and vinegar and continue to cook until the vinegar has evaporated. Remove from the heat and leave to cool.

Cut each chicory head lengthways into sixths, then toss with a little extra virgin olive oil and season with salt and pepper. Heat a griddle pan over a high heat, then quickly mark the cut sides of the chicory on it. If you don't have a griddle pan, do not fret; use an ordinary frying pan instead. The chicory is the crunch element of the salad, so it is important not to overcook it at this stage. Sprinkle it with a little extra Chardonnay vinegar as you take it out of the pan.

Gently toss the chicory with the aubergine and the shallot mixture and tip on to a large platter or bowl. Dot the labneh balls around and serve.

SERVES 4
2 large aubergines
80ml extra virgin olive oil
2 tbsp olive oil
20 fresh curry leaves
1 tsp black mustard seeds
2 pandan leaves
4 large banana shallots, halved and finely sliced lengthways
a thumb-sized knob of fresh ginger, cut into fine strips
6 Medjool dates, pitted and quartered
3 tbsp Chardonnay vinegar, plus a little extra for sprinkling
2 heads of chicory
Maldon salt or other flaky sea salt
black pepper

For the coconut labneh:
500g Greek yoghurt
150ml coconut milk
1 tbsp coconut powder
¼ tsp Maldon salt or other flaky sea salt
1 tbsp sumac
2 tsp Aleppo chilli flakes

SALAD OF SLOW-COOKED OCTOPUS WITH CONFIT ARTICHOKE HEARTS AND SUMAC LAVOSH

I learned this wonderful Italian technique for cooking octopus from Giorgio Locatelli's brilliant book, *Made in Italy: Food and Stories* (Fourth Estate, 2006). We had this dish on our opening menu at The Modern Pantry and it remains a real favourite, yielding a delicately flavoured, firm yet giving meat with accompanying juices, which jellify when left in a cool place. Oh-so-delicious when greedily kept to one side and then later blobbed on to warm, garlicky toast.

The key to success is in the title: 'slow-cooked'. Remain true to that, and this technique will never let you down. I prefer to serve the octopus at room temperature, so I take it out of the fridge 30 minutes before I plan to serve it, but for some, 'room temperature' and 'octopus' are two phrases that should never go together. Feel free to chill or heat the octopus as you so desire.

Place the octopus in a snugly fitting pan with a lid. Scatter all the remaining ingredients around and about, give the pan a good shake, then cover with the lid and turn the heat on low. It should never create more than a gentle simmer. Leave to bubble away gently for 30 minutes or so, then check how it is getting on. Continue to cook for 5–10 minutes, until just tender, checking every so often to ensure that it does not become overdone.

When cooked, take the pan off the heat, remove the lid and leave to cool, then remove the octopus from its juices and store in a container in the fridge until ready to use. Strain the juices through a fine sieve and refrigerate also.

To serve, cut the octopus tentacles into generous-sized chunks. Gently layer the octopus, wedges of artichoke, goats' curd, broad beans, sorrel and pea shoots on a serving dish. Blob the now-jellified octopus juices around and about and serve immediately, with the lemon wedges and shards of lavosh.

SERVES 6

3 Confit Artichoke Hearts
   (see page 128), each cut
   into 6 wedges
175g goats' curd
400g podded broad beans,
   blanched, refreshed in cold
   water, then slipped out of
   their skins
2 bunches of sorrel, shredded
2 punnets of pea shoots
1 lemon, cut into 6 wedges
Sumac Lavosh (see page 218)

For the octopus:
a 1.5kg octopus, thoroughly
   rinsed and patted dry –
   frozen is fine but be sure
   to defrost it fully before
   cooking
5 garlic cloves, crushed
2 large red chillies,
   split lengthways
4 star anise
½ bunch of parsley
   stalks, roughly chopped
125ml extra virgin olive oil

CRISPY SMOKED HAM HOCK WITH MANGO AND PLUM WINE DRESSING

Plum wine is delicious. Buy a bottle, use some for this dressing and drink the rest chilled on ice while you eat it. Very refreshing!

You could also serve this salad with some Spiced Pecans (see page 107) or peanuts sprinkled over it to add a bit of crunch.

First cook the hock. Put it in a large pan, cover with cold water and bring to the boil. Drain and rinse, then return the hock to the pan with the carrot, onion, celery, garlic, peppercorns, star anise and bay leaves. Cover with cold water and bring to the boil again. Reduce the heat to a gentle simmer, cover the pan with a lid and leave to bubble away for an hour or so, until the flesh is tender and comes away from the bone easily. Take off the heat and leave the hock to cool in the poaching liquor.

Remove the hock from the pan and gently prise the flesh away from the bone, removing any small bones and excess sinewy tissue. Leave the fat and skin on unless you have an aversion to it – personally, I like the contrast between the salty, smoky flesh and the gelatinous fatty bits. Chill the meat in the fridge, then dice into 2cm cubes. You can do this up to 2 days in advance.

For the dressing, put all the ingredients except the olive oil in a small pan and simmer until reduced by half. Leave to cool, then whisk in the oil. I don't add salt to this dressing, as the ham hock is usually salty enough, but feel free to add some if you think it is lacking.

Shortly before serving, peel the mango with a potato peeler, slice the flesh away from the stone and cut into chunks. Be sure to spend a minute or two sucking from the stone the final bits of mango goodness that you could not slice off with your knife. Don't be shy, or bothered by the juice dripping down your chin. There is always a flannel to hand, no? One of the secret rewards for the chef.

Heat a little vegetable oil in a frying pan and gently fry the chunks of ham hock until crisp and golden on all sides. Put them into a bowl with the mango, green chilli, coriander, watercress and Thai basil, if using. Toss together with a liberal dousing of the plum wine dressing and serve on individual plates or in a large bowl.

SERVES 4

For the ham hock:
1 smoked ham hock, or 2 if they are on the small side
1 carrot, chopped
1 onion, chopped
1 celery stick, chopped
4 garlic cloves, unpeeled but chopped
8 peppercorns
3 star anise
2 bay leaves
vegetable oil for frying

For the plum wine dressing:
250ml plum wine
80ml mirin
150ml verjus
3 tsp pomegranate molasses
½ tsp coriander seeds
¼ tsp Urfa chilli flakes
10g palm sugar (or dark soft brown sugar)
150ml extra virgin olive oil

To serve:
1 ripe mango
1 green chilli, finely sliced
2 decent handfuls of coriander leaves
3 bunches of watercress, tough stalks removed
10 Thai basil leaves (optional but worth it)

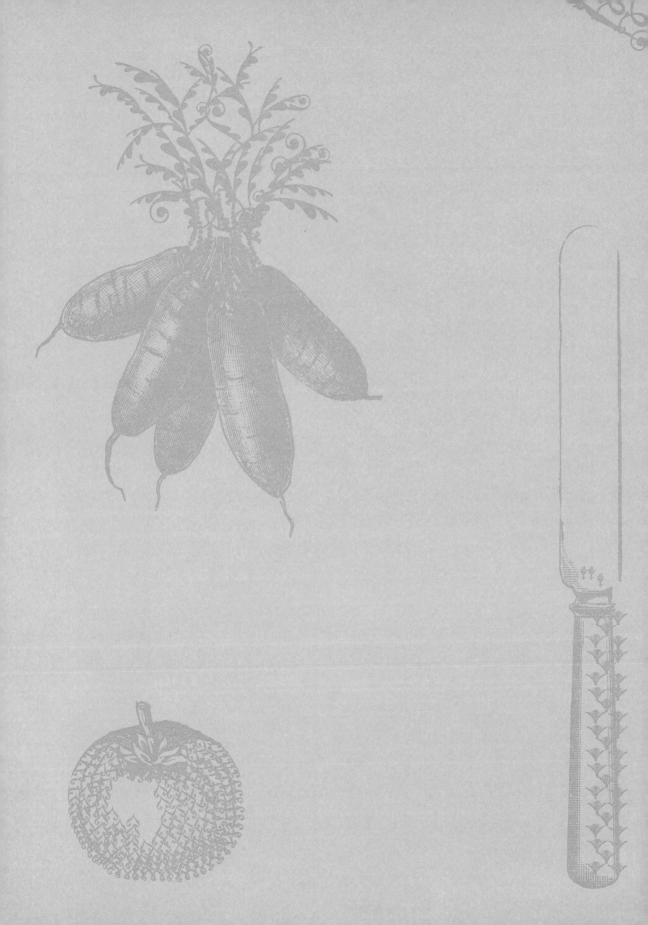

VEGETABLE
DISHES

AUBERGINE DENGAKU

This is my version of a recipe for the classic Japanese dish but with a twist inspired by the fabulous Changa restaurant in Istanbul. There they had the brainwave of mixing tahini into the miso. Delicious indeed. Try substituting 2 tablespoons of tamarind paste for the tahini for a tangy alternative.

These are delicious served either on their own or with Lemongrass-braised Cherry Tomatoes (see page 133) and some crisp, bitter endive leaves.

Slice the aubergines in half lengthways, score the cut side to a depth of 1cm in a crisscross pattern with a sharp knife, then place skin-side down on an oiled baking sheet.

Whisk the Den Miso, tahini and olive oil together, then spread liberally over the flesh of the aubergines. Sprinkle with the sesame seeds, drizzle over a little more olive oil and place in an oven preheated to 180°C/Gas Mark 4. Bake for 20 minutes or so, until the aubergines are cooked through and tender and the miso topping is caramelised. If the topping is caramelising faster than the aubergines are baking, cover with foil and continue to bake until cooked through. Serve immediately.

SERVES 6
3 small aubergines
200ml Den Miso
    (see page 26)
80g tahini
2 tbsp olive oil, plus
    extra for drizzling
2 tbsp sesame seeds –
    a mixture of black
    and white, if you
    have them

BORLOTTI BEAN, PANDAN AND VANILLA STEW

This stew works brilliantly with grilled venison or roast duck. The vanilla and the pandan, often referred to as the vanilla of Asia, complement each other, creating an aromatic, slightly smoky flavour. Omit the pandan if you cannot find it but it is worth seeking out. I have used fresh borlotti beans in this recipe but you could also use flageolet, haricot or rose coco beans.

Pod the borlotti beans. Melt the butter in a pan over a moderate heat. Once it begins to bubble, add the shallots, leek, fennel, carrot and celery and sauté until soft. Scrunch up the pandan leaf with your hands and add this to the pan along with the borlotti beans, bay leaf, white wine and enough water barely to cover the beans. Cover with a lid and leave to simmer gently for 30 minutes or so, until the beans are tender. Once they are all but cooked, slit the vanilla pod open lengthwise and scrape out the seeds. Add both the pod and seeds to the stew and cook for a further 15 minutes. Season to taste with salt and black pepper.

SERVES 4

1kg fresh borlotti beans
  in their pods
50g unsalted butter
2 banana shallots,
  finely diced
1 small leek, finely diced
½ fennel bulb, finely diced
1 small carrot, peeled and
  halved lengthways
1 small celery stick,
  cut into 3
½ pandan leaf
1 bay leaf
100ml white wine
1 vanilla pod
Maldon salt or other
  flaky sea salt
black pepper

Roast Butternut Squash Stuffed with Medjool Date, Cashew Nut and Coriander Couscous

This is a fantastic vegetarian main course, packed with flavour and goodness, that will sate the appetite of even the most committed carnivore! We often serve it for Sunday roast along with all the trimmings or more simply with steamed greens and perhaps some Coconut Labneh (see page 112).

Peel the squash, cut it in half lengthways and scoop out the seeds. Place the squash halves in a shallow roasting dish and sprinkle over the garlic slivers and thyme. Drizzle over the olive oil, pour over the white wine and season with salt and pepper. Cover with foil and roast in an oven preheated to 180°C/ Gas Mark 4 for 25 minutes. Remove the foil and cook for about 10 more minutes, until the squash is tender. This may take a little longer depending on the size of your squash. Check it for doneness as you would a potato and remove from the oven. Leave the oven turned on.

While the squash is cooking, prepare the stuffing Put the couscous or rice flakes in a bowl, pour over 150ml of cold water and leave to soak. Heat the olive oil in a heavy-bottomed pan, add the shallot, leek, cashews, mustard seeds, cardamom, ginger, coconut and curry powder and fry gently until the shallot is soft and the aroma from the spices is making you hungry! If you are using rice flakes, gently drain the excess liquid. Turn up the heat and add the couscous or rice flakes to the pan, stirring thoroughly. Remove from the heat, cover with a lid and leave to cook for 10 minutes. Stir again to fluff up the grains, then add the dates, herbs and lemon juice and season to taste.

Stuff the squash with the couscous or rice flakes and return to the oven for 20 minutes. Serve immediately.

Serves 2
1 small butternut squash
1 garlic clove, very finely sliced
1 tsp chopped thyme
a decent drizzle of olive oil
a splosh of white wine
Maldon salt or other flaky sea salt
black pepper

For the stuffing:
150g instant couscous or medium rice flakes
2 tbsp light olive oil
1 banana shallot or 2 ordinary shallots, finely sliced
1 small leek, finely sliced
100g cashew nuts
1 tsp black mustard seeds
1 cardamom pod, crushed open with the flat of a knife
40g fresh ginger, grated
2 tbsp desiccated coconut
1 tsp hot curry powder
6 Medjool dates, chopped
½ bunch of coriander
½ bunch of flat-leaf parsley
½ bunch of mint
juice of ½ lemon

RED PEPPER, CHERRY TOMATO AND CARDAMOM COCONUT CURRY

This dish is wonderfully aromatic and can be served as a starter or as the main theme in a vegetarian feast. The Quinoa, Tomatillo, Preserved Lemon and Mint Salad (see page 106) and the Roast Cauliflower 'Couscous' (see page 134) are good accompaniments.

Halve the red peppers lengthways, leaving the stalks attached, and carefully remove the seeds. Place three whole cherry tomatoes in each pepper half. Put the peppers in a roasting tin just large enough to hold them.

Melt the butter in a pan over a moderate heat and add the turmeric, garlic, ginger, chilli, curry leaves and spices. Fry until soft and aromatic, then add the coconut cream and cook for 10 minutes or so, until the sauce is rich and thick. Season to taste with salt, then spoon the mixture over the peppers and tomatoes. Roast in an oven preheated to 180°C/Gas Mark 4 for 15 minutes or until the peppers are tender. Transfer the peppers to a platter and scatter with the coriander and spring onions.

SERVES 6 AS A SIDE
DISH OR STARTER

3 large red peppers
18 cherry tomatoes
100g unsalted butter
1 tsp finely chopped fresh
    turmeric (or ¼ tsp
    ground turmeric)
3 garlic cloves, finely chopped
50g fresh ginger, finely grated
1 green chilli, finely chopped
14 fresh curry leaves
1 tsp cumin seeds, toasted
    in a dry frying pan and
    then ground
1 tsp fennel seeds, toasted
    in a dry frying pan and
    then ground
1½ tsp black mustard seeds
6 cardamom pods, crushed
    with the flat of a knife
400ml coconut cream
a bunch of coriander,
    roughly chopped
a bunch of spring
    onions, sliced
Maldon salt or other
    flaky sea salt

BLACK BEAN, STAR ANISE AND COCOA PURÉE

Although the idea of using chocolate in a savoury dish may seem unusual it is one that has been around for centuries. This purée, my take on a recipe I learned from Peter during my days at The Providores, is a brilliant example of how well it can work. Spread the purée on a crostini and top with roast pork belly and quince paste or serve it as you would mash – with roast chicken, duck or venison.

Drain the black beans, put them in a large pan, cover with twice their volume of fresh water and bring to the boil. Drain, rinse under cold water, then return to the pan, covering them once again with twice their volume of water. Add the cinnamon stick, bay leaves and the quartered onion. Bring to the boil, then reduce the heat to a simmer, skimming off the foam that rises to the surface. Leave to bubble away for at least 25 minutes and up to an hour or so, depending on the age of the beans. When they are soft (and they must be soft, or you will end up with unpleasant lumpy bits in your purée), drain them in a colander, reserving a little of their cooking liquid. Remove the cinnamon stick, bay leaves and onion.

In another pan, fry the sliced onion and garlic in the olive oil until they are beginning to caramelise. Add the spices, continue to cook for a minute and then pour in the red wine. When the wine has all but evaporated, add the cocoa powder, chocolate and vinegar, followed by the beans. Season liberally and stir thoroughly.

Process the mixture in batches, using a little of the reserved bean cooking liquid to loosen the purée if needed. It is important that the beans are at least warm at this stage, as it makes the puréeing process much easier and results in a finer, fluffier-textured purée (this is true for any bean purée you may make, such as hummous). If you like, you can add a little extra virgin olive oil now for another layer of flavour and a burst of fruitiness.

SERVES 4

300g dried black beans, soaked overnight in cold water
1 cinnamon stick
2 bay leaves
2 red onions, 1 quartered lengthways and 1 sliced
3 garlic cloves, sliced
125ml olive oil
½ tsp sweet smoked paprika
2 tsp fennel seeds
2 tsp cumin seeds
2 tsp coriander seeds
2 star anise
125ml red wine
2 tsp good-quality cocoa powder
50g dark chocolate (with 70 per cent cocoa solids)
1 tbsp Cabernet Sauvignon vinegar (or ordinary red wine vinegar)
a little extra virgin olive oil (optional)
Maldon salt or other flaky sea salt
black pepper

CONFIT ARTICHOKE HEARTS

The artichoke is one of those vegetables that can be quite daunting when you first decide to take the plunge and, instead of simply boiling it until tender in salty water, retrieve its heart from behind those thorny leaves and fibrous choke. I for one used to think that they were far too difficult to prepare in this way. Although I love confit artichoke hearts, for many years I relegated them to the far-too-troublesome-to-bother-with box.

I now take great pleasure in preparing artichokes (see pages 128–9 for pictures), snapping off their outer leaves, carefully trimming away the tough green exterior and then scooping out the choke to reveal the delicate, topaz-green heart. They are delicious served on bruschetta or in a salad with slow-cooked octopus (see page 115).

Fill a large bowl with cold water and squeeze in the juice of 1 lemon. Snap off the dark-green outer leaves of each artichoke until only the pale, tender inner leaves remain. Using a sharp serrated knife, cut the remaining pointed leaves away to expose the fibres of the choke. Snap off the stem, then use a vegetable peeler to remove any remaining dark green and even out the surface. Finally, use a spoon to scoop out the choke, making sure you remove it all, then drop the artichoke hearts into the acidulated water.

Find a pan that is large enough to hold the artichokes comfortably and has a tight-fitting lid. Add the oil and place over a moderate heat. Pare the zest from the remaining lemons with a vegetable peeler, add to the oil and leave until it begins to sizzle, then add the garlic and cook for 5 minutes or so, until they begin to soften. Add the herbs and leave for a minute longer, then turn up the heat and add the artichokes. Cover with the lid, leave for a minute, then add the juice of the lemons and season liberally with salt and pepper. Stir the chokes around, replace the lid and reduce the heat to low. Leave to simmer for 5 minutes, then check to see if they are tender. They will no doubt need a little longer but the cooking time will depend on the size of the hearts. They should be just cooked through. Once they are tender, remove from the heat and take off the lid. Check the seasoning and leave to cool.

The artichokes can now be stored in their oil and juices for up to a week in the fridge.

3 lemons
4 large globe artichokes
500ml extra virgin olive oil
8 garlic cloves, peeled and
    cut in half lengthways
8 tarragon sprigs
6 thyme sprigs
2 rosemary sprigs
Maldon salt or other
    flaky sea salt
black pepper

LEMONGRASS-BRAISED CHERRY TOMATOES

These are absolutely delicious and go with just about anything.
Make sure you use any leftover juices as a salad dressing, or add
them to a stew, curry or soup.

Gently wash the cherry tomatoes, being careful not to break
them off the stalks. Using a pair of scissors, cut them into
lengths of four or five tomatoes.

Trim the top and bottom of the lemongrass stalk and remove
the outer layer. Place the stalk on a chopping board and crush
with a rolling pin or other suitable implement. This technique
will yield far more flavour than simply chopping it up, as it
bursts open all the juice sacs. Split the lemongrass stalk down
the middle and place in a roasting tin just big enough to hold
the tomatoes. Scatter the ginger, garlic and chilli into the tin
also, then lay the cherry tomatoes on top and sprinkle the
verjus, soy sauce, olive oil and demerara over them. Place
in an oven preheated to 140°C/Gas Mark 1 and cook for
approximately 20 minutes, until the tomatoes just begin to
yield to the heat and their skins split.

Remove from the oven and allow to cool on the tray. These
are best made a few hours before you plan to serve them,
allowing time for the fragrant juices to mingle and be
absorbed by the tomatoes.

SERVES 4
500g cherry tomatoes,
   preferably vine-ripened
   and still on the stalks
1 lemongrass stalk
a small knob of fresh
   ginger, sliced
2 garlic cloves, finely sliced
1 red chilli, split lengthways
100ml verjus
1 tsp soy sauce
100ml extra virgin olive oil
2 tsp demerara sugar

ROAST CAULIFLOWER 'COUSCOUS'

Cauliflower is a vegetable that gets very little press. It is so often relegated to the steamer or, if it's lucky, baked with a gloopy white sauce, a smattering of Cheddar and presented as cauliflower cheese. Don't get me wrong, I love a good cauliflower cheese but there are other possibilities and this is one of them. Roast cauliflower is nutty and sweet and couldn't be simpler to prepare. If you don't have a food processor just serve the roasted florets whole.

Toss the cauliflower, turmeric and fennel seeds together in a roasting dish with a little olive oil and some salt and pepper. Place in an oven preheated to 200°C/Gas Mark 6 and roast for 10 minutes or so, until the cauliflower is beginning to turn golden but is still al dente. The latter is important, as if it is overcooked you will end up with more of a mush than the couscous effect you are aiming for. Remove from the oven and leave to cool.

Tip the cauliflower into a food processor and pulse gently until it resembles couscous. Again, be careful not to overprocess. Transfer to a bowl, stir in the lemon zest, a little extra virgin olive oil and the mint and check the seasoning.

SERVES 4
1 cauliflower, broken
   up into florets
1 tsp finely chopped fresh
   turmeric (or ½ tsp
   ground turmeric)
2 tsp fennel seeds
a little olive oil
grated zest of 1 lemon
extra virgin olive oil
2 handfuls of mint leaves,
   roughly chopped
Maldon salt or other
   flaky sea salt
black pepper

Carrot and Miso Purée

Miso is a fabulous ingredient and one that seems to go with most things, in particular root vegetables, as I have discovered. It adds that elusive layer of umame that can transform an everyday mash into something special. I have used Den miso in this recipe (see page 26) as it adds a little sweetness as well as depth to the flavour of the purée, but if you have not made any I'd recommend you use white miso, which has a more delicate flavour than other misos. If you have another variety of miso to hand, however, that would work fine, you'll simply need to add a little less than you would Den miso as other types of miso will invariably be stronger as they have not had any mirin or sake added to thin them out. You can always add a little more.

If you don't have any carrots or feel like using something else try celeriac, parsnips or butternut squash.

Melt the butter in a heavy-based pan. When it starts to bubble, add the shallots, thyme and ginger and cook until beginning to soften. Add the carrots, cover and cook gently for 10 minutes. Add the cream and a slosh of water and continue to cook over a low heat until the carrots are tender. Remove from the heat, stir in the miso and then purée the carrots in batches in a liquidiser until silky smooth. Season to taste and serve.

Serves 6 generously
125g unsalted butter
150g shallots, diced
1 tbsp chopped thyme
30g fresh ginger, cut into fine strips
750g carrots, finely sliced into rounds
125ml double cream
95g Den miso (see page 26) or white miso
Maldon salt or other flaky sea salt
black pepper

BRAISED RED CABBAGE

My Mum's side of the family is Danish, which meant that growing up involved lots of pickled herrings, *frikadeller* (Danish meatballs) and remoulade – a mixture of mayonnaise and piccalilli that we gaily slathered over innumerable open sandwiches (*Smørrebrød*) – to name but a few of the treats that came with being half Danish. Each year culminated with a Danish feast for Christmas, which we celebrated on Christmas Eve. My Mum, Mormor (grandmother) and us kids would spend the weeks leading up to Christmas baking an array of biscuits and cakes, making decorations for the enormous tree that dominated our sitting room and generally having a lot of fun. On the night, we would gorge on roast pork, brown potatoes (baby new potatoes cooked slowly in sugar and butter), lashings of gravy, a stack of iceberg lettuce leaves with a whipped cream and yoghurt dressing, braised red cabbage and, to finish, *ris a la mande*, a vanilla rice pudding with slivers of almond and whipped cream folded through, and a fresh strawberry sauce.

It was very rich meal to eat in the New Zealand summer but somehow we managed it. Most of the vegetables and fruit came from my grandparents' garden, so I like to think it was a balanced meal.

I loved the braised red cabbage most of all. Mum would make kilos of it and freeze it, so we could continue to eat it throughout the festive season. Believe it or not, it makes a delicious open sandwich on rye bread with sliced leftover boiled new potatoes and a decent grinding of black pepper.

Put all the ingredients into a large, heavy-bottomed pan and mix thoroughly. Cover with a tight-fitting lid and cook over a medium heat for 5 minutes, then reduce the heat to the lowest setting. Leave to simmer, stirring every 10 minutes or so, for about 30 minutes, until the cabbage is tender. Check the balance of acidity to sweetness and adjust to your taste. My Mormor would also add plum juice, which she made every year, to give the cabbage extra fruitiness. You could add a slosh of Ribena concentrate if you don't happen to have any homemade plum juice lurking in your pantry. Just be mindful of its sweetness.

SERVES 4

1 red cabbage, sliced
1 onion, sliced
grated zest and juice
  of 1 small orange
2 Bramley apples, grated
  with the skin on
1 cinnamon stick
1 tbsp ground allspice
250ml Cabernet Sauvignon
  vinegar or good red
  wine vinegar
200g soft brown sugar
300ml apple juice
splash of plum juice or
  Ribena concentrate
  (optional)

CUMIN-ROAST PARSNIP AND PLANTAIN MASH

This may sound like an unusual combination but it really does work, the buttery parsnips and sweet caramelised plantain complemented perfectly by musky toasted cumin seed.

Peel the parsnips, cut them into 2cm-thick rounds and place in a bowl. Peel the potatoes, cut them into slightly smaller pieces and add them to the bowl, along with half the melted butter, the cumin seeds and 100ml of water. Season with salt and pepper. Mix well, then spread the vegetables out in a roasting tin lined with baking parchment and place in an oven preheated to 180°C/Gas Mark 4. Roast for 20–30 minutes, until the potatoes and parsnips are cooked through and have a few crispy bits.

Meanwhile, peel the plantain and cut it into five chunks. Heat 3 tbsp of the remaining melted butter in a heavy-bottomed frying pan over a moderate heat and gently fry the plantain chunks, turning them until golden on all sides and cooked through. Don't leave them unattended or be tempted to crank up the heat, as their high sugar content means they burn easily. Drain the plantain on kitchen paper and chop roughly.

Mash the parsnips and potatoes with a potato ricer, mouli or good old-fashioned potato masher and stir them into the plantain. If you think the mash is a little dry, add the remaining melted butter. Adjust the seasoning to taste.

SERVES 6
1kg parsnips
500g floury potatoes
150g unsalted butter, melted
1¼ tsp cumin seeds, toasted
  in a dry frying pan
1 ripe plantain
Maldon salt or other
  flaky sea salt
black pepper

Fenugreek-roast Sweet Potatoes

Fenugreek is rarely used in Western cooking. It is a spice one generally shies away from when standing in the spice aisle but I have recently begun exploring it in my kitchen. Used sparingly (I have learned to do this the hard way!), it adds an intriguing musky aroma and flavour to savoury and sweet dishes alike.

Scrub the potatoes and cut them into wedges lengthways. Toss with the fenugreek and olive oil, season with salt and pepper, then spread out in a roasting tin lined with baking parchment. Place in an oven preheated to 180°C/Gas Mark 4 and roast for 20 minutes or until soft and golden. Serve immediately.

Serves 6
3 large sweet potatoes
¾ tsp ground fenugreek
2 tbsp olive oil
Maldon salt or other
    flaky sea salt
black pepper

CASSAVA CHIPS

People seem to have a love–hate relationship with this woody-looking African root. Some find it bland and uninspiring but I love it. As chips, it becomes a moreish snack, sprinkled with amchur powder or ground toasted cumin seeds and fine sea salt, and adds an interesting twist to steak and chips. Cassava never strays far from the menu at The Modern Pantry and can usually be found alongside our Grilled Onglet Steak with Tamarind and Miso Marinade (see page 181) or served as a snack with soured cream and Green Pepper and Apple Relish (see page 36).

Cassava is also excellent served as you would a boiled potato, with butter, salt and pepper and perhaps some chopped coriander. The tricky part is handling it when hot. Wearing a pair of rubber washing-up gloves helps protect your hands from the heat while you remove the fibrous core and cut it into chunks. Try this with Hot and Sour Beef Stew (see page 180).

Peel the cassava with a potato peeler. Once you start, you will see that there are several layers – the brown, woody exterior, then a pale pink layer, a creamy-coloured one and finally the crisp, white flesh. It is important to remove all the first three layers. When you have done this, cut the cassava into 5cm lengths, then cut them in half lengthways. Place in a pan, add the table salt and barely cover with cold water. Place the pan on the stove on full heat and cover with a lid. When the water comes to the boil, reduce the heat so that it continues to boil but not as frantically as you would if you were cooking potatoes. Check the cassava after 15 minutes. It will begin to soften and break apart but the cooking time will vary depending on the size of your cassava. You want it softer than a boiled potato, so that when you fry the chips you achieve a light, crisp exterior with a fluffy centre. Overcooking is better than undercooking at this stage. If some pieces are cooked sooner than others, carefully remove them from the pan using a pair of tongs or other suitable implement.

Drain the cassava and leave to cool. Carefully remove the inedible fibrous core, then cut the flesh into chip-like pieces.

Heat the oil to about 180°C in a deep-fat fryer or a large, deep pan. Fry the chips in batches until golden, removing them with a slotted spoon and draining on kitchen paper as you go. Dust with sea salt and your chosen flavourings. Keep the cooked chips somewhere warm while you fry the rest.

SERVES 4

1.5kg cassava
1 tbsp table salt
rapeseed oil for deep-frying
sea salt and flavouring of
   your choice (see above)

SEAFOOD

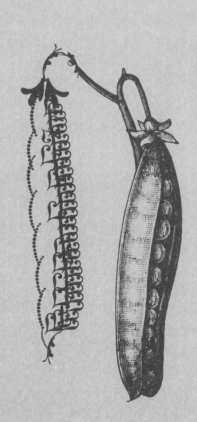

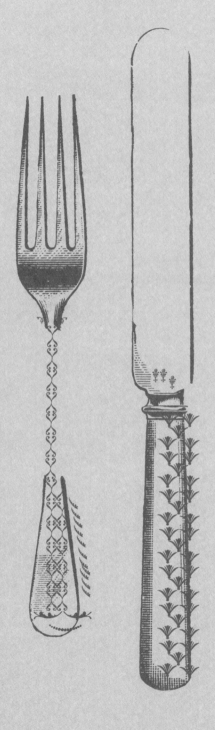

SEA BREAM WITH CRUNCHY SLAW AND COCONUT, ROSE AND LIME DRESSING

To make the dressing, whisk together the coconut milk, lime zest and juice, salt and a few drops of rosewater. I am being a little vague about the rosewater, as in my experience its strength varies from brand to brand. The dressing should be fragrant but not overwhelmed by its perfume.

Prepare the slaw. A Japanese mandoline is ideal for this but a sharp knife is perfectly adequate and good practice. Either way, mind your fingers! Finely slice the fennel crossways and place in a bowl. Squeeze over a little lemon juice to prevent it turning brown. Peel the mango with a potato peeler, cut off 'sheets' of the flesh and then finely slice them. Add to the fennel. Shred the chicory. Core the Granny Smith and slice into fine rounds with the core hole in the middle. Toss all gently together.

To cook the fish, line a baking tray with baking parchment and spread a little olive oil on it. Lay the fillets on it skin-side down, smear half a teaspoon of the sambal over the flesh of each one and season with salt and pepper. Place in an oven preheated to 180°C/Gas Mark 4 and bake for 4–5 minutes, until just cooked.

To serve, place three endive leaves on each plate. Lay the fish on top of this with the sambal side facing up. Add the mint and coriander leaves to the slaw and place a small pile on top of the fish. Spoon over the dressing, garnish with a few extra coriander leaves and serve immediately.

SERVES 6
a little olive oil
6 sea bream fillets,
    scaled and pin boned
3 tsp Smoked Chilli Sambal
    (see page 22)
18 red endive leaves
Maldon salt or other
    flaky sea salt
black pepper

For the coconut, rose
and lime dressing:
250ml unsweetened
    coconut milk
grated zest of 1 lime
juice of 3 limes
½ tsp Maldon salt or
    other flaky sea salt
a few drops of rosewater

For the crunchy slaw:
1 fennel bulb
a few drops of lemon juice
1 mango
1 head of red chicory
1 Granny Smith apple
a handful of mint leaves
a handful of coriander leaves,
    plus extra to garnish

CHERMOULA-BAKED SEA TROUT WITH TAHINI LEMON CREAM

Chermoula is a North-African marinade. Traditionally used with fish and seafood it is heady with spices yet zesty and fresh on account of the lemon and herbs and this combination somehow manages to capture the essence of the sea. My version includes caraway, another anise-like spice, but if you have a particular aversion to caraway feel free to omit it. Try serving with the Quinoa, Tomatillo, Preserved Lemon and Mint Salad (see page 106).

Carefully rinse the sea trout in cold water and pat dry with kitchen paper. Using a sharp knife, slash the skin diagonally three or four times on each side to a depth of 2mm.

Mix the remaining ingredients together in a bowl to make the chermoula marinade, then smother the fish, including the cavity, with it. Leave to marinate for 30 minutes, then either grill on a barbecue or bake in an oven preheated to 180°C/Gas Mark 4 for 15–20 minutes, until the fish is just cooked through.

While the fish is cooking, make the tahini lemon cream. Whisk the tahini, lemon juice and water together, adding more water (or lemon juice) if necessary to achieve the consistency of double cream. Season to taste and serve with the fish.

SERVES 4
1.6kg sea trout, scaled
3 tsp cumin seeds, toasted in a dry frying pan then ground
1 tsp coriander seeds, toasted in a dry frying pan then ground
2 tsp caraway seeds, toasted in a dry frying pan and then ground
1 tsp sweet smoked paprika
¼ tsp dried chilli flakes
1 tbsp finely grated fresh ginger
2 tsp finely grated fresh turmeric (or 1 tsp ground turmeric)
2 garlic cloves, finely chopped
1 banana shallot, finely diced
grated zest and juice of 2 lemons
½ bunch of flat-leaf parsley, chopped
a bunch of coriander, chopped
1 tsp Maldon salt or other flaky sea salt
60ml extra virgin olive oil

For the tahini lemon cream:
125g tahini
juice of 1½ lemons
150ml water
salt

GRILLED MACKEREL WITH SQUID INK MASH AND RED PEPPER AND YUZU DRESSING

I am a big fan of oily fish such as mackerel and sardines, and especially love them grilled. Make sure that your fish is super-fresh and you cook it on the day of purchase, as fish of this nature tends to deteriorate rapidly. I have used prawn oil in the squid ink mash, which adds that wonderful crustacean nuttiness, transforming it into something extra special. You can do without but it is worth the effort.

First make the dressing. Roast the peppers in an oven preheated to 200°C/Gas Mark 6 for 15 minutes or until blackened and blistered. When they are cool enough to handle, peel off the skin, remove the seeds, then place the flesh in a liquidiser or food processor with the mustard, yuzu and lemon zest and juice. Turn on the motor and slowly pour in the oil as though you were making mayonnaise. Season with the black pepper and some salt.

Cook the potatoes in boiling salted water until tender, then drain and mash. Bring the cream to the boil in a pan, add the squid ink and prawn oil and whisk together. Pour the cream over the mash, mix thoroughly and season to taste.

Carefully rinse the mackerel in cold water and pat dry with kitchen paper. Using a sharp knife, slash the skin diagonally two or three times (this helps to ensure even cooking), brush with a little oil and season. To grill the mackerel, lay the fish on top of a hot barbecue or grill pan and cook for about 5 minutes, until the flesh is firm and opaque. Carefully turn over the fish and grill for another 4–5 minutes, until just cooked through. Alternatively, you can bake in an oven preheated to 180°C/Gas Mark 4 for 10–15 minutes. Serve the mackerel with the mash, accompanied by the dressing.

SERVES 4
4 mackerel, gutted
oil for brushing
Maldon salt or other
    flaky sea salt
black pepper

For the red pepper
and yuzu dressing:
2 red peppers
1 tbsp Dijon mustard
2 tbsp yuzu juice
zest and juice of ½ lemon
250ml extra virgin olive oil
¼ tsp black pepper

For the squid ink mash:
1kg floury potatoes,
    peeled and cut into
    chunks
70ml double cream
3 tbsp squid ink
2 tbsp Prawn Oil
    (see page 40)

ROAST COD WITH BEETROOT AND MACADAMIA CRUMBS

I had all but forgotten that macadamia nuts even existed until I was recently given a bag along with some macadamia oil. What a joy! I began experimenting and came up with this dish. The buttery crunch of the delicate macadamia crumbs perfectly complement the sweetness of the cod and musky tang of the shaoxing verjus dressing. If you can't get your hands on any macadamia nuts you could use hazelnuts instead.

You won't need all the crumbs in this recipe but you can freeze the excess. Just flash them through the oven at 140°C/Gas Mark 1 for 10 minutes to crisp them up again. They are also very good tossed through a salad to add texture and flavour.

First prepare the macadamia crumbs. Put all the ingredients except the rapeseed oil in a bowl and mix together thoroughly to make a batter. Heat 3 tablespoons of rapeseed oil in a large frying pan over a moderate heat, then spoon in some of the batter, spreading it out as thinly as you can. Heat about 5cm of oil in another large frying pan and once the batter has set in the frying pan, deep-fry it in the oil in the second pan until golden. Remove with a slotted spoon and drain on kitchen paper. Repeat this process until all the batter has been used, then leave to cool. Blitz to coarse crumbs in a food processor, then store in an airtight container until ready to use.

Peel the beetroot and slice it finely on a mandoline. Place in a roasting tin, add the vinegar and oil, season and mix thoroughly. Cover with foil and place in an oven preheated to 180°C/Gas Mark 4. Bake for 25 minutes or until tender but still with a bit of crunch. Remove from the oven and check the seasoning and acidity, adding a little more salt, pepper or vinegar if required. Leave to cool.

For the dressing, put the Shaoxing, verjus, soy sauce and black cardamom in a pan and cook over a moderately high heat until reduced by about two-thirds of its volume. Remove from the heat and leave to cool. Add the remaining ingredients and blitz with a hand blender to emulsify.

Season the cod on both sides with salt. Heat a little oil over a moderately high heat in a pan that is large enough to hold the cod – use two pans if necessary. Add the butter and when it is melted and bubbling away, put the cod in, skin-side down.

SERVES 6
600g beetroot
100ml Cabernet Sauvignon
  vinegar
90ml extra virgin olive oil
6 pieces of cod fillet, weighing
  about 200g each
a little vegetable oil
a knob of butter
1 lemon
2 bunches of watercress
150g Macadamia Crumbs
  (see below)
Maldon salt or other
  flaky sea salt
black pepper

For the macadamia crumbs:
120g macadamia nuts,
  coarsely ground
1 garlic clove, crushed
3 tsp coriander seeds, ground
3 tsp fennel seeds, ground
2 tsp wattle seeds (optional)
¾ tsp Urfa chilli flakes
10 fresh curry leaves,
  roughly chopped
1 tsp Maldon salt or
  other flaky sea salt
80g rice flour
160ml sparkling water
rapeseed oil for frying

Squeeze over a little lemon juice, reduce the heat slightly and cook for 4 minutes. Using a fish slice, flip the cod over, being careful to keep the skin intact. Cook for a further 3–4 minutes, depending on the thickness of the fillet, until the flesh is just cooked through. It should appear translucent and barely on the verge of flaking apart.

To serve, put a generous pile of beetroot on six plates, lay the fish skin-side up on top and then dress liberally with the Shaoxing dressing and scatter with the macadamia crumbs.

For the dressing:
250ml Shaoxing wine
250ml verjus
60ml light soy sauce
1 black cardamom pod, crushed
2 tsp Dijon mustard
2 tsp salted yuzu juice
50ml light olive oil
50ml macadamia oil

COD WITH CLAMS AND CHORIZO

This is one of my top five favourite dishes to cook when entertaining at home or just for me and it couldn't be simpler or tastier. Eat as it is, or try adding a couple of handfuls of frozen peas to the pan when you add the butter. You could serve it with a little wilted spinach and some boiled new potatoes.

Choose a pan that has a tight-fitting lid and is large enough to hold the fish. Heat the olive oil in it over a moderate heat, add the chorizo and fry gently until the fat begins to run. Push the sausage to the side, turn up the heat and put the cod in, skin-side down. Fry for a minute or so, then add the clams, cherry tomatoes and white wine. Cover with the lid and reduce the heat to moderate again. Cook for 2–3 minutes, being careful not to overcook the fish.

Using a fish slice, carefully transfer the cod and any open clams to 4 serving plates, or one large platter if you prefer. Turn the heat up again and add the parsley and butter or extra virgin oil to the pan. Simmer, shaking the pan from time to time, until the butter has melted and all the clams are open – a minute or two at most. Spoon the sauce over the fish and serve immediately.

SERVES 4

50ml olive oil
100g spicy cooking
  chorizo, diced
4 x 150g pieces of cod fillet
30 fresh clams, scrubbed
10 cherry tomatoes, halved
125ml white wine
a large handful of
  parsley, chopped
a large knob of butter
  or a little extra virgin
  olive oil

PRAWN, CRAB, SUGARSNAP AND AVOCADO SALAD

The provenance of the ingredients we use at The Modern Pantry is very important to me and my team. We spend a fair amount of time researching suppliers and products in an attempt to be as eco-friendly as possible. And with a marine biologist in the family to boot, checking up on my menus from time to time, the pressure is really on!

Happily it is now possible to purchase top-notch sustainably farmed prawns – and yes, you will probably have to pay a little more for them but the benefits by far outweigh the cost. I like to use New Caledonian prawns in this recipe, as they are our prawn of choice at the restaurant, but as long as they are 'green' any other variety will do.

First prepare the sesame cashews. Whisk the egg white for a couple of seconds until just frothy, then add all the remaining ingredients. Spread the mixture evenly on a baking sheet lined with baking parchment and place in an oven preheated to 150°C/Gas Mark 2. Bake for 15 minutes or so, until the nuts are golden. Remove from the oven and leave to cool. The nuts will have stuck together, so gently break them up and then store in an airtight container until ready to use.

Whisk together all the dressing ingredients and set aside.

Quickly fry the prawns in the oil over a high heat for a couple of minutes until just cooked – the shells will be pink when they are ready. Leave to cool and then carefully peel the tails, trying to keep the heads attached.

Slice the red onion as finely as you can and soak in cold water for 5 minutes. Rinse thoroughly and drain.

Blanch the sugar snaps for a minute or so, then refresh under cold running water and drain. Cut into strips lengthways.

Core the iceberg lettuce, gently prise the leaves apart, rinse under cold water and pat dry. Select 4 of the inner cups to act as bowls for the salad. With a sharp knife, shred a couple of the outer leaves, then refrigerate the rest for another occasion. Gently toss together the crab meat, sugarsnaps, avocado, red onion, shredded iceberg lettuce and half the coriander leaves and dress liberally with the yuzu dressing. Layer this with the prawns in each iceberg cup, scatter over some spiced cashews and coriander leaves, and perhaps a little more dressing for good measure. Serve immediately.

Serves 4
16 New Caledonian prawns
1 tablespoon vegetable oil
½ small red onion
12 sugarsnaps
1 iceberg lettuce
200g white crab meat
1 avocado, peeled,
   stoned and diced
leaves from a small
   bunch of coriander

For the sesame cashews:
1 small egg white
1 tbsp caster sugar
1 tbsp sesame seeds
1 tsp nigella seeds
¼ tsp sweet smoked paprika
a large pinch of Maldon salt
   or other flaky sea salt
150g cashew nuts

For the chilli yuzu dressing:
50ml unsalted yuzu juice
grated zest of 1 lime
juice of 3 limes
juice of 1½ lemons
100ml light soy sauce
1 red chilli, finely chopped
50g palm sugar
50ml Shaoxing wine
2 tbsp mirin

SINGAPORE-STYLE WOKKED CRAB

This recipe has been evolving since The Modern Pantry opened.
Every time I cook it, the wonderful aromas transport me back to happy
memories of eating glorious Singaporean food, and although I am certain
it is far from authentic it seems to have the same impact on many of our
diners. It is delicious served with Sticky Coconut Rice (see page 164)
and Turmeric and Cardamom Pickled Lotus Root (see page 22).

Make sure you have plenty of bibs and fingerbowls to hand when
you serve. This is not a dish to eat wearing white!

Put the crabs in the freezer for 2 hours or so before you
cook them. This puts them into a coma and hopefully makes
the whole process less traumatic for them. There are other
ways of quickly and painlessly killing crabs, before you cook
them. Have a look on the internet and you will learn much but
personally I like the idea of going in my sleep and, as I have
no information to the contrary, believe that it is a peaceful
way to go.

Find a pan large enough to hold both crabs comfortably
(if you do not have one, cook the crabs one at a time). Fill the
pan three-quarters full with water, adding 125g of sea salt for
every 5 litres of water, and bring it to a rolling boil. Drop the
crab(s) in and bring back to the boil. Reduce the heat to a very
gentle simmer and start timing. Simmer for 20 minutes, then
pour the contents of the pan carefully into the sink. Refresh
with cold water to help stop the cooking process and wash
off any proteins that have coagulated on the shell.

Once the crabs are completely cool, carefully break off the
claws, then GENTLY crack them with a meat tenderiser or
other appropriate implement and set aside. You want them
to remain intact and you also do not want to spend your entire
crab-eating experience spitting out tiny shards of shell. Flip
each crab belly-side up and remove the pointed flap, then,
holding on to the body of the crab, insert a few fingers into
the holes from whence the claws once protruded and gently
but firmly pull off the top shell. Discard the small stomach sac
– you will find this just behind the mouth and the gills, which
are the featherlike things surrounding the central cavity.
Cut the body into quarters, keeping the legs attached.

SERVES 4
2 x 700–800g live crabs
a little vegetable oil
400ml Prawn Stock
    (see page 42) or other light
    fish or vegetable stock
2 decent handfuls of Thai
    basil leaves
4 spring onions, finely
    sliced into rounds
1 green chilli, finely
    sliced into rounds
leaves from ½ bunch
    of coriander
plenty of sea salt

For the frying paste:
50g fresh ginger
50g garlic
100g shallots
6 red chillies
3 tsp Szechuan peppercorns,
    lightly toasted in a dry
    frying pan
50ml vegetable oil

Put all the ingredients for the frying paste into a food processor and blend until smooth.

Whisk together all the ingredients for the sauce and set aside. Heat the oven to 180°C/Gas Mark 4 and put the top shells in. Heat a little oil in a wok and add the frying paste. Allow to sizzle for a couple of minutes, then add the crab. Depending on the size of your wok, you may have to do this in batches. Toss the crab pieces gently to coat them in the paste and heat through for 5 minutes or so. Add the sauce and the stock and continue to cook, allowing the sauce to reduce a little.

To serve, place the crab in a large bowl with the body shells on top. Scatter the Thai basil, spring onions, chilli and coriander on top and serve immediately.

For the sauce:
3 tbsp light soy sauce
75ml lime juice
75ml fish sauce (nam pla)
2 tbsp Smoked Chilli Sambal
(see page 22)
2 tbsp Tomato Relish
(see page 37)
80g light palm sugar, grated
(or demerara sugar)

POULTRY
AND MEAT

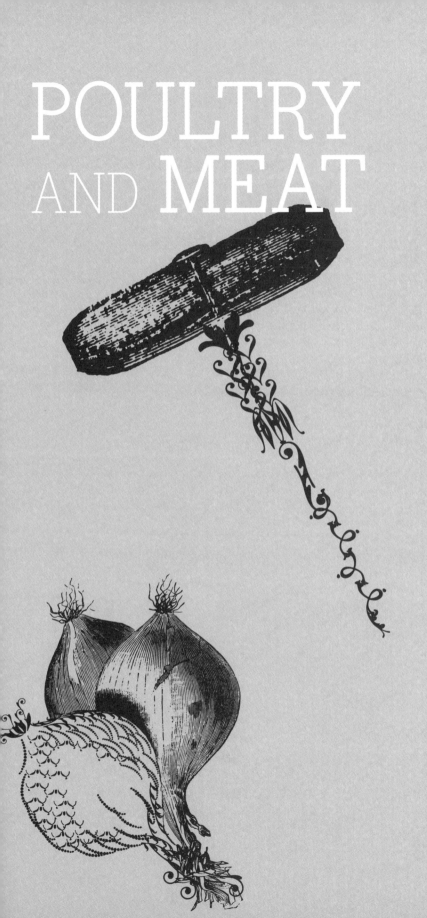

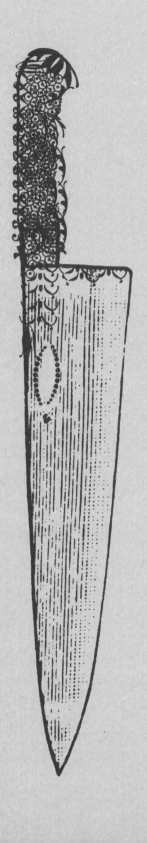

CHICKEN MOLE ROJO WITH TOMATILLO SALSA

This is another wonderful example of how chocolate can be used to brilliant effect in a savoury dish. 'Mole' is the name given to a range of Mexican sauces that are comprised of chillies, nuts and dried fruits, herbs and spices. Some, like this recipe for 'mole rojo', also include chocolate.

Although the list of ingredients may seem daunting the process is actually very simple and the result, a fabulously rich and flavoursome sauce, can be paired with fish as well as meats such as rabbit, guinea fowl and pork.

Traditionally mole is served with rice and tortillas. I like it with ripe plantain, cut into chunks and gently fried in oil until golden all over, and some bitter greens or mustard leaves. I recently served this mole with roast monkfish, substituting the chicken stock for fish stock, and accompanied it with a celeriac gratin as well as the salsa and mole crumbs.

It is not essential to cook the meat in the sauce. You could grill or barbecue your chosen meat or fish and serve the sauce on the side.

Spread the almonds, pumpkin seeds and raisins out on a baking tray and bake in an oven preheated to 160°C/Gas Mark 3 for 10 minutes until the nuts and seeds are golden and the raisins have slightly puffed up. Put the red chilli on a hot griddle or frying pan and cook until charred all over. Trim the stalk.

Lightly toast the sesame seeds, star anise, cloves and cinnamon in a dry frying pan and then grind finely, along with the Urfa flakes. Transfer to a food processor and add the almonds, pumpkin seeds and raisins, the charred red chilli, oregano, thyme, bay leaves and masa harina. Process the mixture to a fine, aromatic powder. Remove 2 tbsp of the powder from the processor and set aside.

Char the tomatillos, onion and garlic under a hot grill. This will take 5–10 minutes, depending on the efficiency of your grill. Add them to the food processor and blitz again until you have a consistent mass.

Transfer this to a large pan, whisk in the chicken stock and bring to the boil. Reduce the heat and simmer for 15 minutes, then whisk in the chocolate and season to taste.

Heat the oil in a large frying pan, add the chicken pieces and brown thoroughly over a high heat, seasoning them as you go. Place in an ovenproof dish, pour over half the mole sauce (you won't need the rest but you can freeze it for up to two

SERVES 4

60g unskinned almonds
50g pumpkin seeds
50g raisins or sultanas
1 large red chilli
3 tbsp sesame seeds
2 star anise
10 cloves
1 cinnamon stick
1 tbsp Urfa chilli flakes
3 tsp fresh oregano
2 tsp thyme leaves
2 large bay leaves
50g masa harina or
    stale breadcrumbs
6 tomatillos, husks removed
1 onion, roughly chopped
10 garlic cloves, peeled
1 litre chicken stock
80g dark chocolate
    (with 70 per cent
    cocoa solids), chopped
1 tbsp vegetable oil
1 chicken, jointed into 8
Maldon salt or other
    flaky sea salt
black pepper

months), cover with foil or a lid and bake at 180°C/Gas Mark 4 for 30 minutes or so, until the chicken is cooked through.

Meanwhile, make the salsa. Remove the papery husks from the tomatillos, wash them then dice the flesh finely and put in a bowl. Cut away the skin and pith from the limes, then finely dice the flesh, avoiding the tough central core. Add to the bowl along with all the remaining ingredients, mix well and season to taste.

When the chicken is done, remove it from the sauce and keep warm. Pass the sauce through a coarse sieve and then through a fine one, pushing firmly down on the contents of the sieve each time with the back of a ladle. You want to extract as much liquid and flavour as possible. Return the sauce to the pan, adjust the seasoning then gently bring to the boil. Put the warm chicken on a serving plate, pour the sauce over it and sprinkle over the reserved powder. Serve immediately with the salsa.

For the tomatillo salsa:
250g tomatillos
2 limes
1 shallot, finely diced
50ml extra virgin olive oil
25ml muscatel vinegar
a handful each of chopped
   coriander, chervil and mint

COCONUT AND PANDAN DUCK LEG CURRY WITH STICKY COCONUT RICE

Heat 2 tablespoons of the oil over a moderate heat in a large, heavy-bottomed frying pan. Thoroughly brown the duck legs in it on all sides, seasoning as you go, then remove from the pan and set aside. Pour off the excess fat, then add a little of the chicken stock to the pan, scraping and stirring to deglaze. Reserve these juices.

Heat the rest of the vegetable oil in a large casserole over a moderately high heat and add the laksa paste, star anise, coriander seeds, cinnamon and chilli. Fry until soft, fragrant and beginning to caramelise. Add the lemongrass, lime leaves, ginger, onion, garlic and coriander stalks and continue to fry for 5 minutes. Now add the tamarind, palm sugar and fish sauce and cook until the palm sugar has dissolved. Stir in the coconut milk, the remaining chicken stock, the deglazing juices and three pandan leaves. Put the duck legs into the pot, gently pushing down to submerge them in the curry sauce, and bring to the boil. Don't worry if there is not enough liquid to cover the duck legs completely, as they will give out plenty of liquid as they cook. Cover with a tight-fitting lid or foil and transfer to an oven preheated to 140°C/Gas Mark 1. Braise for 2 hours or until the meat is tender and comes easily away from the bone.

Carefully remove the legs from the sauce and keep somewhere warm. Pass the curry first through a coarse sieve and then through a fine one, pushing firmly down on the contents of the sieve each time with the back of a ladle. You want to extract as much liquid and flavour as possible. Return the sauce to the pan and adjust the seasoning, adding soy sauce or lime juice as your palate requires. The sauce should have a tangy, hot edge to it with a subtle layer of pandan. If the pandan has not come through, scrunch up another leaf and add it to the sauce. Put the duck legs back in the sauce and reheat gently.

To make the sticky coconut rice, rinse the rice and put it in a pan with the coconut milk and the water and salt. Bring to the boil, then reduce the heat to low and cook, stirring once or twice, for 15–20 minutes, until the rice is just cooked through.

Transfer the curry to a serving dish and garnish with the coriander leaves, spring onions and crispy shallots. Serve with the sticky coconut rice.

SERVES 6
80ml vegetable oil
6 duck legs, excess
    fat trimmed away
400ml chicken stock
125g Laksa Paste
    (see page 23)
4 star anise
1 tbsp coriander seeds,
    coarsely ground
1 cinnamon stick, broken up
1 red chilli, chilli
2 lemongrass stalks, trimmed,
    bashed and chopped
5 kaffir lime leaves
100g fresh ginger, chopped
1 large red onion, sliced
4 garlic cloves, chopped
a large bunch of coriander,
    stalks chopped, leaves
    reserved
125g tamarind paste
30g palm sugar, grated
40ml fish sauce (nam pla)
400ml unsweetened
    coconut milk
3–4 pandan leaves, scrunched
soy sauce, to taste
lime juice, to taste
a bunch of spring onions,
    sliced
Crispy Shallots (see page 25)
Maldon salt or other
    flaky sea salt
black pepper

For the sticky coconut rice:
400g glutinous white rice
500ml unsweetened
    coconut milk
500ml water
1 tsp salt

GRILLED ROSE MARINATED QUAIL WITH ROAST PLUMS AND ROSE YOGHURT

A delicate and fragrant dish, this makes a fantastic starter but if you prefer to serve it as a main course, just double the quantities.

Using scissors, remove the spine of each quail and lay the birds out flat. Whisk together all the ingredients for the marinade. Thoroughly coat the quails with the mixture and leave to marinate in the fridge for at least an hour or up to one day.

Preheat the oven to 140°C/Gas Mark 1. Lightly oil a roasting dish just large enough to accommodate the plums and put them in it skin-side down. Sprinkle over the umeshu, extra virgin olive oil and demerara sugar. Season with salt and pepper and roast for 15 minutes or so, until the plums are tender but still hold their shape. Remove from the oven and set aside.

Put the lemon juice, rosewater and petals into a small pan and heat very gently for just a minute or two without letting it boil. Remove from the heat and leave to cool. Strain through a fine sieve into the yoghurt, pushing down gently with the back of a ladle to extract as much colour and flavour as possible from the petals. Take half of these rose petals, chop roughly, add to the yoghurt and season with salt. If you think the yoghurt needs a little more rose flavour, add more rosewater.

Remove the quails from the fridge at least 30 minutes before you plan to cook them to bring them up to room temperature. Fire up your barbecue, or heat a ridged grill pan, and once the flames have died down and the coals are good and hot, lay the quails on it, spine-side down. Grill for 5 minutes, then turn over and grill for another 4–5 minutes, until the birds are just cooked through but still pink and juicy. Remove from the grill and leave to rest somewhere warm, covered in foil, for 5 minutes. Bear in mind that they will continue to cook a little even when taken off the heat. Serve with the yoghurt and plums.

SERVES 6 AS A STARTER
6 quails
6 plums, halved and stoned
100ml umeshu (plum) wine
50ml extra virgin olive oil
1 tbsp demerara sugar
1 tbsp lemon juice
40ml rosewater
2 tsp rose petals
200g Greek yoghurt
Maldon salt or other
   flaky sea salt
black pepper

For the marinade:
100ml rosewater
4 tbsp olive oil
50ml pomegranate molasses
4 tbsp umeshu (plum) wine
1½ tsp cumin seeds, toasted
   in a dry frying pan and
   then ground
2 tsp dried rose petals
   (optional)

SMOKY ROAST POUSSINS WITH TAHINI, ORANGE AND SOY DRESSING

This marinade works just as well on other birds and on pork chops; it is particularly tasty when barbecued. Fenugreek-roast Sweet Potatoes (see page 138) make a great accompaniment.

Remove the spine of each poussin with a pair of scissors and lay the bird out flat. Whisk all the ingredients for the marinade together and thoroughly coat the poussins in it on both sides. Cover and refrigerate for at least an hour and up to one day.

To make the dressing, put all the ingredients except the vegetable oil into a liquidiser and blend to make a paste. Gradually pour in the oil with the motor running, as you would for mayonnaise. Adjust the seasoning by adding more soy if necessary.

Heat a little oil in a frying pan over a moderate heat and lay the birds in it, skin-side down (you can cook them in batches, washing the pan in-between if it has burnt). Thoroughly brown the birds, then turn them over and place in a roasting tin large enough to hold all four. Transfer to an oven preheated to 180°C/Gas Mark 4 and roast for 30–40 minutes, until the birds are cooked through and the juices run clear. Serve with the dressing.

SERVES 4
4 small poussins
vegetable oil

For the marinade:
100ml hoisin sauce
4 tsp sherry vinegar
4 tsp soy sauce
4 tsp sesame oil
grated zest of ½ orange
2 tsp black (or white)
  sesame seeds
1 tsp sweet smoked paprika
½ tsp chipotle powder or
  dried chilli flakes
2 garlic cloves, crushed

For the dressing:
100g tahini
grated zest and juice of
  1 small orange
juice of ½ lemon
1 thumb-sized knob of
  fresh ginger
3 tbsp dark soy sauce
2 tbsp rice wine vinegar
2 tbsp mirin
1 tbsp Tomato Relish
  (see page 37)
1 tbsp sesame oil
½ tsp Szechuan peppercorns,
  lightly toasted in a dry
  frying pan then ground
100ml vegetable oil or
  light olive oil

PERSIAN-SPICED PORK SKEWERS WITH SWEET TOMATO YOGHURT

This Persian spice mix is my pared-down version of a recipe from a dear Iranian family friend, Reza Parvin. The original, which he makes in bulk for us to use at The Modern Pantry, has 29 different spices – hence the need to pare it down! It is a wonderfully spicy, fresh and fragrant marinade that works equally well with chicken, lamb or fish.

If you are using wooden skewers, soak them in water for 30 minutes or so before using. This helps prevent them burning when you put them in the oven or on the grill.

Remove any sinew from the pork fillet, then cut it into 2cm cubes and put it in a bowl.

For the spice mix, blitz the spices, salt, lemon juice, ginger, garlic, vegetable oil and three-quarters of the fresh coriander together in a food processor to make a paste. Tip it on to the diced pork and mix well. Leave to marinate for at least 1 hour and up to 24 hours.

Make the sweet tomato yoghurt by whisking the tomato relish and yoghurt together and seasoning with salt and pepper to taste.

Thread the meat on to 8 skewers, then place in an oven preheated to 180°C/Gas Mark 4 and bake for 10 minutes (or cook them on a barbecue or ridged grill pan). Serve immediately, scattered with the remaining coriander and accompanied by the sweet tomato yoghurt.

SERVES 4
600g pork fillet

For the spice mix:
1½ tsp paprika
1½ tsp ground fennel seed
1 tsp dried chilli flakes
¾ tsp ground coriander
¾ tsp ground turmeric
¾ tsp garam masala
¾ tsp curry powder
¼ tsp ground cardamom
¼ tsp ground black pepper
½ tsp ground ginger
½ tsp ground cinnamon
1 tsp salt
juice of 1 lemon
1 tablespoon finely
   chopped fresh ginger
1 large garlic clove, peeled
50ml vegetable oil
a bunch of coriander,
   roughly chopped

For the sweet
tomato yoghurt:
2 tbsp Tomato Relish
   (see page 37)
150g plain yoghurt
Maldon salt or other
   flaky sea salt
black pepper

SLOW-ROAST PORK BELLY WITH COX'S APPLE, SOUR CHERRY AND FENNEL CHUTNEY

Eating a slowly roasted pork belly, oozing unctuous goodness, with perfectly crisp crackling makes me feel very, very happy. I almost always brine my pork belly a day ahead of cooking it. As well as allowing you to add flavours that penetrate deep into the meat, brining ensures that the end product is always super-moist. I highly recommend you give it a go but of course it isn't a prerequisite to a fantastic pork belly roast.

Using a very sharp knife, score the skin of the pork belly as finely as you can, being careful not to cut into the flesh too much. You just want to open the surface of the skin, and the closer the scoring, the better the crackling will be – you could ask your butcher to do this for you.

In a container large enough to hold the belly, put the salt, paprika, star anise, fennel seeds and bay leaves. Pour in enough cold water to cover the belly and whisk to dissolve the salt. Place the pork belly in the brine skin-side down and leave in the fridge to soak for at least 24 hours (and up to 36 hours).

If you do not have the time to brine the belly in this way, simply grind the spices and bay leaves in a coffee grinder or spice mill and add 3 tablespoons of salt. Mix together and then rub the mixture over the belly. Marinate for 12 hours and roast as below.

To roast, remove the belly from the brine, rinse and pat dry. Place the potatoes in a roasting tin, rest the belly on top, skin-side up, pour in 200ml of water and then place in an oven preheated to 140°C/Gas Mark 1. Roast for about 1½–2 hours. The timing will depend on the thickness of the belly but it will take at least this long. You will know it is ready when a fork pushed into the flesh comes away easily. When the pork is done, crank up your oven to 200°C/Gas Mark 6 and cook for an additional 8–10 minutes. This should make the crackling bubble up and go crisp. A trick we use at the restaurant, though, when the crackling refuses to behave itself, is to heat up a little oil in a heavy-bottomed frying pan. When it is hot, lay the belly in it skin-side down and it will puff up. If the surface of the crackling is uneven, just press it down where it is not touching the pan.

Leave the pork belly to rest for 15 minutes, then carve and serve with the potatoes it was cooked on and the chutney.

SERVES 6
2.5kg piece of pork belly
200g table salt
1 tbsp smoked paprika (if not available, use ordinary paprika)
4 star anise, crushed
2 tbsp fennel seeds, crushed
3 bay leaves
4 medium potatoes, cut in half lengthways
Cox's Apple, Sour Cherry and Fennel Chutney (see page 38), to serve

ROAST LEG OF LAMB AUNTY SOSS'S WAY, WITH SPICED ROAST PARSNIPS AND CARROTS AND CRISPY ROAST POTATOES

The marinade for this lamb is something my Aunty Soss taught me (Soss for sausage, although her name is actually Sonja … Don't ask!). She calls it legless lamb, which I hasten to add is not a reference to the condition of the beast it came from, although the irony is hard to escape! Soss would marinate a boned leg of lamb in this marinade overnight then grill it on the barbeque. Her barbeques were legendary. On arrival guests were served a delicious but potent G&T with a slice of sweet Meyer lemon from her garden along with 'nibbles', which is what Soss terms anything that is crisp enough to be piled with a topping or scooped through bowls of dip more or less intact. This was followed by other tasty morsels served with plenty of perfectly chilled white wine and ice cold beer. Eventually the lamb and vegetables would be served, usually cooked to perfection but sometimes just a little too charred or more than a little undercooked depending on whether she had forgotten to take them off the barbeque or put them on! Hence the title, legless lamb.

A handful of polenta can be added to the coating for the potatoes, a suggestion – and a very good one at that – from Dougal, one of my managers at The Modern Pantry. It works a treat, giving you even more crunch for your buck.

As you are now well aware I like to use spices, and adding a twist to simple things without too much extra effort is what they are all about. These roast vegetables are no exception: grating a knob of ginger or chopping a chilli adds minutes to your workload but I can guarantee you it's worth doing.

Trim the excess fat and membrane from the leg of lamb. With a sharp paring knife, pierce the flesh all over. Mix all the marinade ingredients together and smother the leg of lamb in it, making sure you rub the marinade into the cuts in the flesh and any other natural crevices. Place the lamb in a plastic food bag with the marinade and leave in the fridge for at least 6 hours, ideally for 24 hours.

Make a vegetable trivet by roughly chopping the carrot, celery, onion and garlic and placing them in a roasting dish that will hold the lamb snugly. Put the lamb on top of this, add the white wine and a slosh of water and place in an oven preheated to 225°C/Gas Mark 7. Roast for 20 minutes, then reduce the heat to 180°C/Gas Mark 4 and roast for another 40 minutes to 1 hour,

SERVES 6
2.5kg leg of lamb
1 carrot
1 celery stick
1 onion
a few garlic cloves
250ml white wine
Maldon salt or other flaky
   sea salt
black pepper
Cox's Apple, Sour Cherry
   and Fennel Chutney (see
   page 38) or Tomato Relish
   (see page 37), to serve

depending on how pink you like your meat, basting with the pan juices as you go.

Meanwhile, prepare the other vegetables. Parboil the potatoes, then drain in a colander and toss about a few times to make the outsides fluffy. Mix with the onion seeds, Urfa flakes, rosemary, garlic and an extra generous slosh of oil. You probably don't want to hear this but in my experience the more generous the slosh, the more abundant the golden crispy bits. I'll leave it to you. Season liberally, then put in the oven with the lamb and roast for 30–35 minutes, turning from time to time, until golden and crisp.

Toss all the ingredients for the carrots together in a roasting tin, season with salt and pepper and put into the oven with the lamb, cooking for about 35 minutes, until tender and golden. Do the same for the parsnips, but they take a little less time to cook so put them in 10 minutes later.

When the lamb is cooked to your liking, remove it from the oven, cover loosely with foil and leave somewhere warm to rest for 15 minutes or so. You can make a gravy, if you like, with the pan juices from the lamb. Or don't. I have never been very good at that! Just strain them as they are into a jug and skim off the excess fat. Slice the lamb and arrange with the roast vegetables and maybe something green if you fancy it. Serve with the chutney or relish.

For the marinade:
200g natural yoghurt
80ml olive oil
1½ tbsp finely chopped preserved lemon zest (see page 34), or grated fresh lemon zest
juice of 1 lemon
1 tbsp chopped thyme
3 tsp cumin seeds, toasted in a dry frying pan and then ground
1 tsp sweet smoked paprika
3 garlic cloves, chopped
2 tsp salt (3 if using fresh lemon zest)
1 tsp black pepper
1 tsp dried chilli flakes

For the potatoes:
12 small to medium potatoes, peeled
1½ tsp nigella (black onion) seeds
2 tsp Urfa chilli flakes
2 tsp chopped rosemary
6 garlic cloves, sliced
slosh of vegetable oil

For the carrots:
6 sweet carrots, quartered lengthways
a thumb-sized knob of fresh ginger, finely chopped
½ green chilli, chopped
2 tbsp extra virgin olive oil

For the parsnips:
6 parsnips, quartered lengthways, cores removed if woody
1 tsp black mustard seeds
2 tsp finely chopped fresh turmeric (or ½ tsp ground turmeric)
a handful of fresh curry leaves
2 tbsp extra virgin olive oil

GRILLED LAMB CHOPS WITH SMOKED ANCHOVY SALSA

In the year leading up to opening The Modern Pantry I worked for the lovely Vaughan family in Herefordshire, cooking during shoot weekends over the game season. I would arrive on Fridays at noon then cook my way through the weekend, which culminated in Sunday roast. It was a brilliant and creative time for me and is when I came up with this wonderful tangy yet delicate salsa.

First make the salsa. Heat the oil in a frying pan and gently cook the lemon zest and garlic in it until soft. Add the salted anchovies and continue to cook, mashing up the anchovies with a wooden spoon, until they have disintegrated. Add the lemon juice, take the pan off the heat and pour the contents into a bowl. Leave to cool, then add the smoked anchovies and chopped herbs. Season and add a little more lemon juice if you think it needs it.

Turn the grill on to a high heat. Brush the lamb chops with oil, season with salt and pepper and grill for 3–4 minutes on each side until done to your liking. Serve with the salsa.

SERVES 4
8 lamb chops
a little oil for brushing
Maldon salt or other
    flaky sea salt
black pepper

For the smoked anchovy salsa:
4 tbsp extra virgin olive oil
20g lemon zest, pared off in
    strips with a vegetable
    peeler and roughly chopped
3 garlic cloves, chopped
60g salted anchovies
juice of ½ lemon
125g smoked anchovies,
    roughly chopped
a bunch of chervil, chopped
½ bunch of flat-leaf parsley,
    chopped

SEARED OLOROSO-MARINATED VENISON LOIN WITH BONE MARROW AND HIJIKI JUS

This dish goes brilliantly with Carrot and Miso Purée (see page 135) or Cassava Chips (see page 140).

Mix together all the ingredients for the marinade, then smother the venison in it. Place the lot in a plastic food bag and leave to marinate in the fridge for 6–8 hours. Be sure to remove the venison from the fridge at least 30 minutes before you plan to cook it, to bring it up to room temperature.

While the venison is marinating, soak the marrowbone in cold, salty water for at least 2 hours. This helps to draw out the blood as well as making it easier to extract the marrow. Drain the bones, then remove the marrow by gently but firmly pressing down on the narrower end of it. Slice the marrow into 1cm-thick rounds, then put them in a tub of fresh cold, salty water until ready to use.

To make the jus, melt the butter in a pan over a moderate heat. Once it is happily bubbling, add the shallot, garlic and thyme and cook gently for about 5 minutes, stirring from time to time, until softened and sweet. Add the chicken stock and Oloroso, bring to the boil, then reduce the heat, skimming off any foam that may have risen to the surface. Leave to simmer for 5 minutes or so, then stir in the bone marrow and hijiki.

Remove the venison from the marinade and season with black pepper. Heat a little oil in an ovenproof frying pan over a moderately high heat and add the venison. Fry for 2–3 minutes, until well browned underneath, then turn the loin over. Cook for an additional 2 minutes, then transfer to an oven preheated to 200°C/Gas Mark 6 and cook for 4–5 minutes. The cooking time will vary depending on how thick the loin is but you want it very pink. Anything more and it will have a vile, mealy texture – a totally disrespectful way to treat such a fine cut of meat!

Remove the venison from the oven and transfer to a plate. Cover with foil and leave to rest somewhere warm for 10 minutes, then slice and serve with the bone marrow and hijiki jus.

SERVES 4
650g piece of venison loin
   or short loin, sinew removed
a little vegetable oil

For the marinade:
150ml Oloroso sherry
50ml olive oil
2 tsp chopped thyme
½ tsp sweet smoked paprika
½ tsp Aleppo chilli flakes
1 shallot, super-finely sliced
2 garlic cloves, sliced
1 tsp Maldon salt or other
   flaky sea salt
black pepper

For the bone marrow
and hijiki jus:
5 pieces of marrowbone,
   5cm long
a small knob of butter
1 shallot, finely diced
1 garlic clove, finely sliced
1 tsp chopped thyme
300ml Dark Chicken
   Stock (see page 39)
75ml Oloroso sherry
1 tbsp Soy-braised Hijiki
   (see page 43)
salt

HOT AND SOUR BEEF STEW

Serve this hearty stew with mash (at The Modern Pantry we serve it with Cumin-roast Parsnip and Plantain Mash, see page 137), and steamed greens of your choice.

Very lightly dust the beef in well-seasoned flour and then fry in a little vegetable oil over a moderate heat until well browned all over. This browning process is very important, caramelising the meat and juices and thereby adding that rich, luscious, meaty flavour that all good stews require. Set the browned meat aside. Pour the red wine into the pan and stir and scrape the base with a wooden spoon to deglaze. Reserve these pan juices.

Heat a little more vegetable oil in a large, heavy-bottomed casserole over a moderate heat. Add the laksa paste and fry, stirring frequently, until aromatic. Add the onion, leek, carrot, celery, fennel, ginger and lemongrass and continue to cook, stirring from time to time, until softened and sweet. Stir in the palm sugar, tamarind paste, fish sauce, black cardamom and star anise and cook for a further 3–4 minutes. Add the beef, the reserved pan juices and the stock. The liquid should nearly cover the beef but not quite. Cover with a tight-fitting lid or foil and place in an oven preheated to 140°C/Gas Mark 1. Cook for 1¾–2 hours, until the meat is tender and the gelatinous vein running through the middle is soft and unctuous.

Remove the meat from the liquor and leave in a warm place. Allow the liquor to cool for a moment or two and then carefully pass it through a fine sieve, using the back of a ladle to push the juices and some of the fibres from the vegetables through. Rotating the ladle in a circular motion whilst gently pushing down will give the best results. Once you have extracted as much juice as you can from the vegetable matter, return the liquid to the pot and check the balance of flavours – it should be tart, yet soft and well rounded. A little more palm sugar or tamarind, and some salt may be necessary.

Return the beef to the pan and reheat gently. Serve immediately.

SERVES 4

1kg piece of beef feather blade, sinew removed, cut into 4 steaks
a little plain flour, seasoned with salt and pepper, for dusting
vegetable oil for frying
250ml red wine
4 tbsp Laksa Paste (see page 23)
1 onion, diced
1 leek, sliced
1 carrot, sliced
1 celery stick, sliced
1 small fennel bulb, sliced
100g fresh ginger, sliced
2 lemongrass stalks, trimmed and bashed
40g palm sugar, grated
80g tamarind paste
1 ½ tbsp fish sauce (nam pla)
2 black cardamom pods, crushed
3 star anise
1 litre beef or chicken stock
Maldon salt or other flaky sea salt

GRILLED ONGLET STEAK WITH TAMARIND AND MISO MARINADE

Onglet steak, otherwise known as skirt or hanger steak, is one of my favourite cuts of beef for both flavour and texture. Forming part of the diaphragm of the animal, it protects the liver, kidneys and other internal organs, which in turn impart some of their rich, offaly flavour.

This Modern Pantry classic uses tamarind and sweet/salty Den miso to enhance these flavours, delivering a tangy steak with plenty of umame goodness. We serve it with Cassava Chips (see page 140) and Lemongrass-braised Cherry Tomatoes (page 133) or Tomato Relish (page 37).

One last thing: be careful not to overcook the steak. This cut really must be eaten rare to medium-rare. Anything more and you will be left with a stringy, inedible mass. And yes, you will be expected to chew!

Mix all the marinade ingredients together, pour them over the steak and leave to marinate for at least 3 hours, preferably overnight.

Heat a griddle or a heavy-based frying pan over a high heat until hot but not smoking (if the pan is too hot, the outside of the meat will burn before it has cooked enough). Brush the steaks with the oil and season. Cook for 2–4 minutes on each side, depending on thickness. Transfer them from the pan to a rack, cover with foil and leave to rest in a warm place for up to 10 minutes. This helps the meat to 'relax' and maximises taste and tenderness.

SERVES 6

6 x pieces of onglet steak,
  each weighing,150–180g,
  trimmed
50ml olive oil
Maldon salt or other flaky
  sea salt
black pepper

For the marinade:
125g tamarind paste
70ml Den Miso (see page 26)
2 garlic cloves, finely sliced
1 tsp chopped thyme

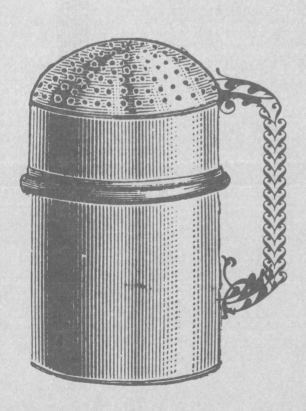

DESSERTS

WATTALAPAM BREAD AND BUTTER PUDDING WITH SPICED ROAST APRICOTS

My dear friend, Elaine Murzi, 'Queen of Tarts' at The Modern Pantry, came up with this inspired version of a bread and butter pudding. Wattalapam is a Sri Lankan dessert rather like a flan, but heady with spice and coconut, which together with the croissants lift this classic pudding to a whole new level. Serve with Coconut Sorbet (see page 204), if you like.

Place the apricots cut-side up in an ovenproof dish in which they fit snugly, putting a knob of the butter on top of each one. Mix the sugar with the spices, sprinkle it over the apricots and then squeeze over the lemon juice. Bake in an oven preheated to 160°C/Gas Mark 3 for about 20 minutes, until tender. They can be served warm or at room temperature (if you don't plan to eat them in the next couple of hours, store in your fridge until ready to serve; they will keep for up to three days).

To make the bread and butter pudding, butter a deep-sided 30 x 20cm ovenproof dish. Put the coconut milk, spices and sugars in a pan and heat gently until the sugar has melted. Remove from the heat and leave to cool, then whisk in the double cream and eggs.

Slice each croissant in three horizontally. Peel the bananas and slice them in three lengthways. Place a layer of croissant in the buttered dish, then a layer of banana. Pour over a third of the coconut custard mix and a third of the melted butter. Repeat the process twice.

Put the dish in a roasting tin, then pour hot water into the tin around the dish. Place in an oven preheated to 150°C/Gas Mark 2 and bake for 30–40 minutes, until the custard has set. Remove from the oven and serve with the roast apricots and Coconut Sorbet (see page 204).

SERVES 6
400ml coconut milk
1 cinnamon stick
2¼ tsp ground allspice
2¼ tsp ground cardamom
seeds of 1 vanilla pod
50g caster sugar
75g pale palm sugar, grated
   (or demerara sugar)
200ml double cream
4 large eggs
6 stale croissants
3 ripe bananas
100g unsalted butter,
   melted, plus extra for
   greasing

For the spiced roast apricots:
6 ripe apricots, halved
   and stoned
30g unsalted butter
2 tbsp sugar
¼ tsp ground star anise
¼ tsp ground cinnamon
⅛ tsp ground cardamom
juice of 1 lemon

RHUBARB, LEMONGRASS AND SAGO COMPOTE WITH CLOTTED CREAM

This is a wonderful combination and is refreshingly light and aromatic.
If you don't have time to make the meringues it is pretty good on its own,
although what is stewed fruit without cream?

Bring a medium pan of water to a rolling boil and pour in the sago in a thin stream, as you would polenta, stirring constantly to prevent it sticking together. Simmer for 10 minutes, then remove from the heat, cover with a lid and leave to stand for 15 minutes, until translucent. Transfer to a fine sieve and refresh under the cold tap. Keep to one side.

Slit the vanilla pod open lengthwise and scrape out the seeds. Put the pod and seeds in a pan with the white wine, lemongrass and sugar. Bring to the boil, then reduce the heat and simmer for 5 minutes. Add the rhubarb, cover with a lid and cook gently for 4–5 minutes, until the rhubarb is tender. Remove from the heat and leave to cool completely, then stir in the sago. Serve the compote with Muscovado Meringues and a dollop of clotted cream. It also goes brilliantly with the Coffee Cream on page 192.

SERVES 4
80g sago
1 vanilla pod
200ml white wine
1 lemongrass stalk,
    trimmed bashed and
    split lengthwayse
100g white sugar
500g rhubarb, cut into
    5cm lengths

To serve:
Muscovado Meringues
    (see page 192), to serve
clotted cream or Coffee
    Cream (see page 192)

SESAME PANNA COTTA
WITH SALTED PISTACHIO PRALINE

First make the pistachio praline. Put the sugar in a small, heavy-based pan, add a tablespoon of water and place over a low to medium heat until melted. Raise the heat and cook until it forms a dark-golden caramel. Add the nuts and salt and remove from the heat. Pour the mixture on to a parchment-lined baking tray and leave to cool. When it is completely cold and hard, smash into small pieces using a rolling pin or by blitzing in a food processor. Store in an airtight container until ready to use.

For the panna cotta, bring the milk, cream and sugar to the boil in a pan and then take off the heat and whisk in the tahini and vanilla seeds. Meanwhile, soak the gelatine leaves in a bowl of cold water for about 5 minutes, until soft. Squeeze out excess water from the gelatine and add the leaves to the milk mixture. Stir until dissolved, then leave to cool completely. Pass through a fine sieve, then fill eight dariole moulds almost to the top with the mixture and refrigerate until set – approximately 3–4 hours, depending on the efficiency of your fridge.

To serve, quickly dip the moulds in a bowl of hot water to loosen the panna cotta and invert immediately on to serving plates. Sprinkle with the salted pistachio praline.

SERVES 8
800ml milk
600ml double cream
120g caster sugar
130g tahini
seeds of 1 vanilla pod
5 gelatine leaves

For the praline:
100g caster sugar
140g pistachios,
   lightly toasted
½ tsp Maldon salt or
   other flaky sea salt

STEAMED KUMQUAT MARMALADE PUDDING

I love this marmalade recipe, which comes courtesy of Christine Manfield's Paramount Desserts, my bible when I first took the plunge into a full-time pastry position at The Sugar Club after it opened.

You will need to have made the marmalade before you can embark on making the pudding but once it's made it will keep for up to a year in the fridge. It is excellent on toast but also works wonders folded through vanilla ice cream or spread on a chocolate roulade served with whipped cream.

To make the marmalade, halve the kumquats and pop out the seeds, but keep them. Put the kumquats in a container, add enough water just to cover and then leave overnight.

The next day, put the kumquats and their water into a large pan with the sugar. Tie the seeds into a small piece of J-cloth and add them too (you need these for their pectin, which will help the marmalade set). Bring to the boil, stirring to dissolve the sugar, then reduce the heat and simmer gently for about 30 minutes, until the mixture has the consistency of a soft jam. Spoon into sterilised jars and seal...or don't seal and eat!

Now you can make the pudding. Thoroughly butter an 18cm ring mould and spread the kumquat marmalade over its base. Cream the butter, sugar and lemon zest together until pale and fluffy, then beat in the eggs one by one. Sift in the flour and baking powder and gently fold them in.

Spoon the mixture into the ring mould, then cover tightly with foil. Place it in a roasting tin and pour enough hot water into the tin to come about half way up the side of the mould. Carefully transfer to an oven preheated to 190°C/Gas Mark 5 and bake for 40–50 minutes or until a skewer inserted in the centre of a pudding comes out clean. The cooking time may vary according to the shape of your mould.

Take off the foil, run a knife round the edges of the pudding, invert on to a serving plate and gently remove the mould. Serve immediately, with lashings of cream.

SERVES 8
8 tbsp Kumquat
   Marmalade (see below)
150g unsalted butter,
   softened
150g caster sugar
grated zest of 2 lemons
4 eggs
150g plain flour
½ tsp baking powder
cream, to serve

For the marmalade:
500g kumquats
250g white sugar

MUM'S APPLE TORTE

My Mum often made this cake when she had guests for dinner. It was my favourite childhood dessert and conjures up many happy memories for me: the slightly crispy, toffeeish exterior, the warm, moist interior flavoured with apple and marzipan, and last but by no means least, the masses of soft whipped cream that accompanied it. What could be better than a slice of Mum's apple torte baked in her red and white Danish enamel ring mould? And still the only possible answer to that is two.

Lightly beat the egg, add the sugar and almond extract and beat again. Stir in the apple slices. Sift the flour, baking powder and salt together, then stir them into the apple mixture.

Thoroughly butter an 18cm ring mould – and I mean thoroughly – then carefully spoon in the batter, trying not to get any on the edges. If you don't have a ring mould you can use an 18cm cake tin or six small dariole moulds. Do not fill the tin more than two-thirds full. Bake in an oven preheated to 160°C/Gas Mark 3 for 25 minutes or until the cake is golden and a skewer inserted into the centre comes out clean.

Remove from the oven and leave to cool for 15 minutes, then carefully turn the cake out on to a plate. Serve while still warm, accompanied by the whipped cream – although it is pretty all right when cold, too.

SERVES 6

1 egg
170g white sugar
½ tsp almond extract
2 tart eating apples,
    such as Granny Smith,
    peeled, cored and sliced
55g plain flour
1 tsp baking powder
a pinch of salt
butter for greasing
250ml whipping cream,
    softly whipped

Honey-roast Pear, Chestnut and Oat Crumble

Chestnut flour is eaten throughout Italy, but especially in Tuscany, where it is most famously used in *castagnaccio*, a dense, flat cake of which I am a great fan. Here I have used chestnuts as well as chestnut flour, and together they add a sweet nuttiness to the crumble topping.

Place the butter, sugars, flours and chestnuts in a food processor and pulse to coarse crumbs. Tip into a bowl, add the oats and mix well, then chill. At this stage you could even freeze the crumble topping for another day, if you wish.

Peel, core and dice the apples and pears, put them into a large bowl, then sprinkle over the cinnamon and cardamom. Pour over the honey and mix well. Tip the mixture into an ovenproof dish large enough to hold it comfortably, then pile on the crumble topping. Place in the centre of an oven preheated to 180°C/Gas Mark 4 and bake for 40 minutes or so, until the fruit is cooked and its juices are happily bubbling around the edges of your perfect, golden crumble. Remove from the oven and leave to cool for 5 minutes or so, then serve. For me, runny cream is all that is required.

Serves 6
2 large Bramley apples
6 pears
2 tsp ground cinnamon
1 tsp ground cardamom
100ml honey

For the topping:
125g unsalted butter
70g soft brown sugar
60g granulated sugar
60g chestnut flour
60g self-raising flour
200g cooked chestnuts
   (vacuum packed
   or canned is fine)
70g rolled oats

MUSCOVADO MERINGUES WITH COFFEE CREAM AND CAPE GOOSEBERRIES

This is an old favourite of mine and, if you make smaller meringues, a perfect cocktail-party dessert canapé. The beauty of it is that you can make the meringues up to a week in advance and store them in an airtight container until you need them. All you have to do to serve is whip the cream, spoon it on to the meringues and top each one with a Cape gooseberry.

First make the meringues. Put the egg whites, icing sugar and lemon juice into the bowl of an electric mixer and beat on high speed for 15 minutes. The meringue should be thick and glossy, and if you taste the mixture it should be silky smooth. Fold the muscovado sugar through the meringue.

Using a large spoon, blob the mixture on to two parchment-lined baking sheets. With the back of a dessertspoon, make a bowl-shaped dip in each meringue. This provides a cup to hold the cream. Place in an oven preheated to 100°C/Gas Mark ¼ and bake for 2 hours. Remove from the oven and leave to cool.

When the meringues are cool and you are ready to serve them, whip the cream to soft peaks with the instant coffee. Halve the Cape gooseberries. Spoon the coffee cream on to the meringues and top each one with half a gooseberry

SERVES 8
300ml whipping cream
1¾ tbsp cooled instant coffee
1 punnet of Cape gooseberries

For the muscovado meringues:
4 egg whites
300g icing sugar
1 tbsp lemon juice
80g muscovado sugar

CHOCOLATE LIQUORICE DÉLICE WITH COCOA CHILLI WAFERS

The idea for this dessert came to me after a visit to my lovely Aunty Kimmi in Denmark. With a liquorice allsort already in my mouth, I greedily stuffed in a chocolate and the result was a taste sensation I have never forgotten.

Don't be put off this dessert if you don't like liquorice. For some reason, the combination of liquorice and chocolate has won over the most hardened liquorice haters.

Liquorice is available to buy online at www.thespicery.com

SERVES 6
370ml milk
330ml double cream
25g liquorice juice stick, broken into pieces, or 25g good-quality liquorice paste
5 egg yolks
120g caster sugar
250g dark chocolate (70 per cent cocoa solids), chopped
3 pink grapefruit, segmented
250ml whipping cream, softly whipped

For the cocoa chilli wafers:
45g unsalted butter
25g liquid glucose
20ml Cabernet Sauvignon vinegar
40g caster sugar
8g cocoa powder
2g pectin powder
15g dark chocolate (70 per cent cocoa solids)
¼ tsp Maldon salt or other flaky sea salt, plus extra for sprinkling
¼ tsp sweet smoked paprika (optional)
¼ tsp Aleppo chilli flakes

To make the délice, put the milk, cream and pieces of liquorice juice stick (but not the liquorice paste, if you are using that) into a pan and bring to boiling point. Meanwhile, whisk the egg yolks and sugar together in a bowl. Gradually whisk in the hot milk mixture, then pour back into the pan and cook gently, stirring constantly, until thickened. Pour this hot custard over the chopped chocolate and whisk gently until completely dissolved and smooth. Stir in the liquorice paste, if using, then pass through a fine sieve into a bowl. Press a piece of baking parchment gently on to the surface to prevent a skin forming and leave to cool. Chill for at least 2 hours, preferably overnight.

To make the cocoa chilli wafers, put the butter, glucose and vinegar in a small pan and heat gently until the butter has melted. Add the sugar, cocoa powder and pectin and bring to the boil. Continue to boil for 2 minutes, stirring occasionally, then remove from the heat and whisk in the remaining ingredients. Using a palette knife, spread the mixture as thinly as possible on a baking sheet lined with a silicone baking mat or a piece of baking parchment. It will look gloopy but don't worry; it will spread as it bakes. Place in an oven preheated to 180°C/Gas Mark 4 for 9 minutes, until it's a glossy, bubbly mass, then remove from the oven and sprinkle a little more salt on top. Leave until cool and crisp (if it is not crisp, put the tray back in the oven for a few minutes longer). Gently break the wafer into large shards and store, layered with baking parchment, in an airtight container until needed.

To serve, place a scoop of the chocolate liquorice délice on each plate. Lay a grapefruit segment on top and then a wafer and spoonful of whipped cream. Serve immediately.

Hokey Pokey Ice Cream

This is a Kiwi classic – honeycomb folded through vanilla ice cream.
There are many schools of thought as to how thick, how golden and
how aerated one's hokey pokey should be if it is to be used in ice cream.
I have witnessed several heated debates at The Modern Pantry between
connoisseurs but when all is said and done, as long as it is not burnt,
honeycomb folded through vanilla ice cream is always a delight. We
serve it as it is or as an affogato – with a hot espresso poured over.

If you don't happen to have an ice cream machine, or the time or
inclination to make the ice cream, just buy a tub of good-quality vanilla
ice cream, soften it and fold your hokey pokey through. Et voilà!

First make the ice cream base. Put the milk, cream and half
the sugar in a heavy-bottomed pan and bring to the boil.
Meanwhile, whisk the remaining sugar with the egg yolks and
vanilla seeds. When the milk and cream mixture is boiling, take
it off the heat and gradually whisk into the yolks. Be careful not
to add it too quickly or you will end up with a lumpy, curdled
mass. Put the pan back on the stove over a low heat, pour the
mixture into it and cook, stirring constantly with a wooden
spoon, until the custard thickens (don't let it boil or it will
curdle). Strain through a fine sieve and leave to cool.

While the ice cream base is cooling, make the hokey pokey.
Line a deep baking tin with baking parchment. Gently melt the
sugar, golden syrup and liquid glucose together over a medium
heat in a large, heavy-based pan. The large pan is important,
as the mixture will at least quadruple in volume when you add
the bicarbonate of soda. When the sugar has melted, turn the
heat up high and leave to boil, stirring intermittently, until its
already-golden colour begins to deepen and you get just that
whiff of caramelisation. Be careful not to take it any further
than this, as the mixture will continue to cook once removed
from the heat and your seemingly perfectly caramelised hokey
pokey will rapidly take a turn for the worse! If you have a
thermometer, take it to 140–150°C.

Sift the bicarbonate of soda and tip it into the pan. Stir
vigorously for 15 seconds or so, then immediately remove
from the heat and pour out into the parchment-lined tin, being
extremely careful not to get any of the sweet, molten lava on
you. The mixture should continue to bubble and grow in the tin.
Resist the temptation to prod it or move the tin, as the bubbles
will collapse and you will end up with flat hokey pokey.

Serves 8

For the vanilla ice cream:
500ml milk
500ml double cream
200g caster sugar
10 egg yolks
seeds from ½ vanilla pod

For the hokey pokey:
245g caster sugar
55g golden syrup
95g liquid glucose
12g bicarbonate of
soda, sifted

Once the mixture is cool and hard, enjoy the fun of smashing it up with the utensil of your choice (I favour a rolling pin). Store in an airtight container until ready to use.

Churn the custard in an ice cream machine according to the manufacturer's instructions. Fold 230g of hokey pokey chunks through the ice cream and freeze for a good 30 minutes or so before serving.

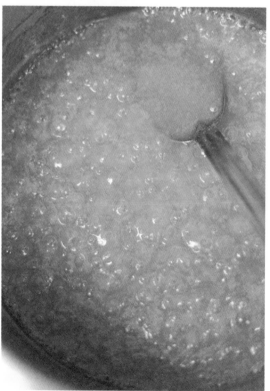 

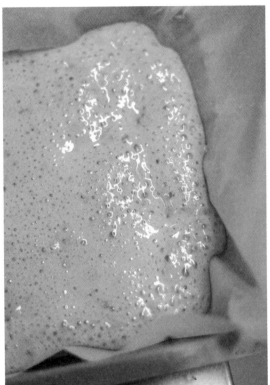

MALT ICE CREAM

This delicious ice cream was developed by Shuna Fish Lydon, pastry-chef extraordinaire, during her stage at The Modern Pantry. It is the sort of ice cream that is hard to stop eating once begun and will impress the pants off your friends should you actually manage to share it with them.

Put the milk, cream, demerara and soft brown sugar in a heavy-bottomed pan and bring to the boil. Meanwhile, whisk the white sugar and egg yolks together in a bowl. When the milk and cream mixture is boiling, remove from the heat and gradually whisk it into the yolks. Be careful not to add it too quickly or you will end up with a lumpy, curdled mass.

Put the pan back on the stove over a low heat, pour in the mixture then cook, stirring constantly with a wooden spoon, until the custard thickens; don't let it boil or it will curdle. Whisk in the malt extract and salt until dissolved, then strain through a fine sieve and leave to cool. Chill thoroughly, then churn in an ice cream machine according to the manufacturer's instructions.

SERVES 8
750ml milk
500ml double cream
100g demerara sugar
50g soft brown sugar
85g white sugar
8 egg yolks
185g malt extract
¼ tsp Maldon salt or
    other flaky sea salt

Rye Bread Ice Cream

The Dane in me rears its head again! When I was a child my Mormor made a dessert that consisted of a bowl of tart stewed apples topped with a layer of custard then a layer of soft whipped cream, and lastly, the crowning glory of the pudding, a layer of the lightest crispy breadcrumbs, which she had pan-fried to caramelised perfection in butter and sugar. Oh how I loved those breadcrumbs... and the cream... heaven! The pudding was all the more special because the custard was made with real vanilla beans which my Aunties would bring from Denmark when they visited every couple of years (the world was a far larger sphere in those days and vanilla was a hard thing to come by in New Zealand).

It was later, thinking about that dessert while making ice cream, and with a loaf of rye bread to hand, that I came to this. Enjoy!

Blitz the rye bread to coarse crumbs in a food processor. Melt the butter over a medium heat in a pan large enough to hold the crumbs in a single layer. Add the caraway seeds. When they begin to toast and smell aromatic, add the rye crumbs and sugar. Fry gently for about 10 minutes, until the sugar has dissolved and the crumbs are golden and becoming crisp. Stir in the salt, then spread the crumbs out on kitchen paper and leave to cool.

Churn the ice cream base in an ice cream machine according to the manufacturer's instructions. Fold in three-quarters of the crumbs and freeze until firm. Serve with the extra rye crumbs sprinkled on top.

Serves 8
200g rye bread
30g unsalted butter
1 tsp caraway seeds
2 tbsp demerara sugar
¼ tsp Maldon salt or
   other flaky sea salt
1 quantity of Vanilla Ice
   Cream Base (see page 196)

SORBETS

Few things are as refreshing as sorbet and you'll be pleased to know,
if you don't already, that they are refreshingly easy to make. If you do
not have an ice cream machine, you can always freeze as you would a
granita. Pour the liquid mixture into a shallow tray, place in the freezer,
then stir and break up the ice crystals with a fork regularly throughout
the freezing process. Or simply freeze in ice-lolly moulds. Of course, the
texture won't be quite the same as it would had it been churned, but it
will still taste great.

SORBET SYRUP

This basic stock syrup goes into most of our sorbets, the liquid glucose
yielding a smooth, creamy texture. A general rule of thumb is two parts
fruit purée to one part sorbet syrup but you still need to pay attention to
acidity, flavour etc. and make adjustments as you go.

Place all the ingredients in a heavy-based pan and bring to the
boil, stirring to dissolve the sugar. Reduce the heat and simmer
gently for 5 minutes, then leave to cool. Store the syrup in the
fridge, where it will keep for several weeks.

MAKES 600ML
375ml water
260g white sugar
115g liquid glucose

RASPBERRY ROSE SORBET

Put the raspberries in a large pan with the sorbet syrup, bring
to the boil and simmer gently for 3–4 minutes, until cooked.
Pass through a fine sieve, discarding all but 1 tablespoon of the
raspberry seeds. Stir in the lemon juice and rosewater, adding
more to taste if needed. Chill thoroughly, then churn in an ice
cream machine according to the manufacturer's instructions.

SERVES 8
1kg raspberries
  (frozen ones are fine)
450ml Sorbet Syrup
  (see above)
juice of 1 lemon
1 tbsp rosewater

BANANA GALANGAL SORBET

I came up with this sorbet combination years ago when I was working at The Sugar Club. I think I may have been eating a banana, then chopped up a piece of galangal, and the pungent, floral aromas complemented each other so perfectly I decided to give it a go. It turned out to be a match made in heaven. I hope you like it, too.

Put the sorbet syrup and galangal in a small pan and bring slowly to the boil, then remove from the heat and leave to infuse. Once cool, strain, discarding the galangal.

Blitz the bananas in a food processor with the lemon juice and rum, then stir into the infused sorbet syrup with the water. Chill thoroughly before churning in an ice cream machine according to the manufacturer's instructions.

SERVES 6
250ml Sorbet Syrup
  (see page 203)
50g galangal, finely sliced
450g very ripe bananas
juice of ¼ lemon
100ml good-quality
  aged rum
50ml water

COCONUT SORBET

Whisk all the ingredients together, then churn in an ice-cream machine according to the manufacturer's instructions. This is excellent served with Wattalapam Bread and Butter Pudding (see page 184).

SERVES 6
700ml coconut milk
400ml Sorbet Syrup
  (see page 203)
juice of 2 limes,
  grated zest of 1
juice and grated
  zest of 1 lemon

Chocolate Truffles

This is our super-simple, bog-standard truffle recipe. If you wish to add flavours, such as cardamom or coffee for example, infuse them in the cream by bringing the cream and flavouring slowly to a simmer, then leaving to cool before straining and adding to the chocolate and butter. Adding ground spices directly to the truffle mix gives an unpleasant texture. Adding toasted nuts or dried fruit, on the other hand, gives a great texture.

If you wish to add alcohol, use no more than 35ml or the truffles will become grainy. Other than that, have fun experimenting. I have given a few of my favourite flavours overleaf to get you started.

Break up the chocolate and put it in a bowl with the butter. Place the bowl over a pan of barely simmering water, making sure the water doesn't touch the base of the bowl. When the chocolate and butter have melted, remove from the heat and stir in the double cream. Refrigerate for an hour or so, until set.

Fill a jug with hot water and dip a melon baller into it. Use the hot melon baller to scoop out balls of truffle mix and then tap them out on to a tray, dipping the baller in and out of the hot water as necessary. (If you don't have a melon baller, you can simply scoop out the truffle mix with a teaspoon and roll it between the palms of your hands. You will have to wash your hands several times throughout the process and work fast so that the chocolate does not melt.)

Chill the truffles in the freezer for 30 minutes or so. Melt the additional 150g chocolate in a bowl set over hot water, as above. Sprinkle a tray liberally with cocoa powder. Drop three or four truffles at a time into the melted chocolate, then remove them with a fork – or, if you happen to own such a thing, a chocolate dipping fork – gently shaking them to remove the excess chocolate. Drop the truffles on to the cocoa-lined tray and leave to set for 20 seconds before gently shaking to coat with the cocoa powder.

Store the truffles in an airtight container in the fridge until ready to serve but be sure to remove them at least half an hour in advance to bring them to room temperature.

Makes about 12
250g dark chocolate
   (70 per cent cocoa
   solids), plus an extra
   150g for dipping
50g unsalted butter, diced
125ml double cream
best-quality cocoa
   powder for coating

MANUKA HONEY AND PEANUT BUTTER TRUFFLES

Elaine's answer to Reece's peanut butter cups. Omit the butter
from the recipes on page 205 and add 150g smooth peanut
butter plus 1½ tbsp Manuka honey and a pinch of sea salt to the
chocolate as you melt it. The truffle mix will set a bit softer than
the basic recipe. Dip in melted chocolate, then roll in crushed
salted peanuts.

HONEYCOMB TRUFFLES

Make the basic truffle mix on page 205, folding through 150g
smashed-up hokey pokey bits (see page 196) before you chill it.
Once set, scoop and dip as above.

TONKA BEAN AND CHILLI TRUFFLES

Using a nutmeg grater, grate one tonka bean and put it in a
small pan with 125ml of double cream and ¾ teaspoon of dried
chilli flakes. Bring slowly to the boil, then remove from the
heat and leave to cool completely. Follow the basic recipe on
page 205, replacing the plain cream with the tonka and chilli-
flavoured cream.

BREAD AND BAKING

Soda Bread

This recipe was passed on to me by my good friend, Sue Lewis (of 15-minute Preserved Lemon fame, see page 34), and is most definitely the best soda bread I have come across. It has the perfect balance of savoury and sweet, a wonderful texture and, besides being superb when freshly baked, any leftovers make wonderful croûtons for salads or crostini to top with something delicious. Once you have mastered the basic recipe, try adding seeds and spices, such as pumpkin and sunflower seeds, fennel and caraway, for a different texture and flavour.

Heavily butter one large (or two small) loaf tins and coat with oats. Mix the oats, flours, salt and bicarbonate of soda together in a large bowl. In another bowl, whisk the buttermilk, whole milk, melted butter, honey and treacle together. Pour this into the dry ingredients and mix thoroughly.

Spoon the mixture into the loaf tin, filling it no more than three-quarters full. Wet your hands and flatten the mixture out, then sprinkle with more oats. Place in an oven preheated to 200°C/Gas Mark 6 and bake for 20 minutes. Reduce the temperature to 160°C/Gas Mark 3 and continue to bake for 20–30 minutes, until a skewer inserted into the middle of the loaf comes out clean. If you are not 100 per cent sure, bake it for another 10 minutes. It will do no harm.

Remove the bread from the oven and leave to cool in the tin for 15 minutes, then turn out on to a wire rack and leave to cool completely … although there are not many things better than soda bread still warm from the oven slathered in butter. Yes, I love butter!

Makes 1 large or
2 small loaves
40g porridge oats, plus extra for coating the tin and sprinkling
50g jumbo oats
225g wholemeal flour
225g unbleached strong white bread flour
3 tsp table salt
2 tsp bicarbonate of soda
300ml tepid buttermilk
120ml tepid whole milk
50g unsalted butter, melted, plus extra for greasing the tin
50g honey
2 tbsp treacle

FIG ANISE BREAD

Add the yeast to half the tepid water with the sugar and leave for about 10 minutes to dissolve and foam. Meanwhile, coarsely process the figs in a food processor with the remaining water.

Put the flour, salt and star anise in a large bowl and mix well. Add the yeast mixture to the flour, along with the puréed figs and the oil. Mix with a wooden spoon to get the dough going, then roll up your sleeves and bring the dough together with your hands. Turn it out on to a lightly floured surface and knead for 5 minutes or so, until smooth and elastic. Place in a bowl, cover with cling film or a clean tea towel and leave in a warm place for about an hour, until doubled in volume.

Tip the dough out on to a work surface and knock it back, then cut in half and shape into two long, thin loaves. Roll each loaf in polenta to coat and transfer to a baking sheet. Slash along the length of each loaf with a sharp knife, cover as before, and leave to rise again for an hour or so, until doubled in volume.

Bake the loaves in an oven preheated to 220°C/Gas Mark 7 for 10 minutes, then reduce the heat to 180°C/Gas Mark 4 and bake for a further 15 minutes or until the bread sounds hollow when tapped underneath. Transfer to a wire rack and leave to cool.

MAKES 2 LOAVES
10g fresh yeast or
   1 tsp dried yeast
250ml tepid water
2 tbsp sugar
400g dried figs
320g unbleached strong
   white bread flour,
   plus extra for dusting
¾ tsp table salt
2½ tsp ground star anise
50ml light olive oil
polenta for dusting

CORNBREAD

Butter a large loaf tin and dust with polenta. Sift the polenta, flour, bicarbonate of soda and baking powder into a large bowl, then thoroughly mix in the sugar and the salt. Whisk the eggs with the buttermilk and melted butter, then whisk them into the dry ingredients. Pour the batter into the loaf tin, sprinkle a little more polenta on top and place in an oven preheated to 180°C/ Gas Mark 4. Bake for 20 minutes or so, until a skewer inserted into the centre comes out clean.

Remove from the oven and transfer to a wire rack to cool. Serve with lashings of butter.

MAKES 1 LARGE LOAF
butter for greasing
175g polenta, plus extra
    for dusting
150g plain flour
⅛ tsp bicarbonate of soda
¼ tsp baking powder
50g soft brown sugar
1 tsp Maldon salt or
    other flaky sea salt
2 large eggs
300ml buttermilk, at
    room temperature
60g unsalted butter,
    melted, plus extra
    to serve

OATCAKES

To me these are everything an oatcake should be – crisp and flakey, buttery and full of oaty goodness.

Sift the plain flour, sugar, salt, baking powder and bicarbonate of soda into a large bowl, then tip the mix into a food processor. Add the wholemeal flour and butter and pulse until the mixture has a crumb-like consistency. Tip this back into the mixing bowl, add the jumbo and porridge oats and, using your hands, mix until evenly combined. Add the egg whites and gently mix again until the dough just comes together, as though you were making shortcrust pastry. Don't overmix or the oatcakes will be tough. Divide the dough into three, shape into flattish discs, then wrap in cling film and chill for 30 minutes.

Once the dough has rested, roll it out on a lightly floured work surface or between two sheets of baking parchment until it is 5mm thick. Cut into squares or circles or whatever shape you like, place on a parchment-lined baking sheet, 1cm apart, and bake in an oven preheated to 160°C/Gas Mark 3 for about 12 minutes, until pale golden. Remove from the oven and, using a palette knife or fish slice, carefully transfer the oatcakes to a wire rack to cool. Store in an airtight container for up to a week.

MAKES ABOUT 36
160g plain flour, plus
   extra for dusting
½ tbsp caster sugar
¾ tsp table salt
¼ tsp baking powder
½ tsp bicarbonate of soda
160g wholemeal flour
360g cold unsalted
   butter, diced
180g jumbo oats
180g porridge oats
6 egg whites

POTATO, ROSEMARY AND NIGELLA FOCACCIA

There are few things more satisfying in life (or at least in kitchen life) than making bread, and once you get into the swing of it the process becomes almost therapeutic. Each loaf is always slightly different from the one before depending on the freshness of the yeast, the moisture and gluten content of the flour, how long the dough was proved for and at what temperature you baked the loaf. The more you make bread the easier it becomes and the better it gets. Keeping your dough quite moist and making sure you prove it properly each time will go a long way towards baking fantastic bread but I really believe that approaching the task with a relaxed and happy disposition is the key to success!

Add the yeast to the tepid water and leave to dissolve and foam. This should take about 10 minutes. Put the flour and salt in a large bowl and mix together. Add the yeast mixture, along with the oil, and mix with a wooden spoon to form a dough, then roll up your sleeves and bring the dough together with your hands. Shape it into a ball.

Sprinkle your work surface liberally with flour and knead the dough, pushing it away from you with the palms of your hands and then pulling it back again. Don't worry if it feels sticky; I find oiling my hands as I go works well and stops me adding too much flour. Keep kneading until the dough becomes elastic and springs back when you press it with your thumb. You could do the kneading in an electric mixer if you have a dough hook. Put the dough back in the bowl, cover with a tea towel and leave somewhere warm to rise. It will take at least 40 minutes. When it has doubled in size, beat the dough down with your hands and then leave it to rise until doubled again. Tip it out on to your work surface and flatten it out with your hands into a focaccia-esque shape.

Liberally oil a large baking sheet, or two if necessary, lay the dough on top and use the palms of your hands to squish it out as much as you can. It will keep bouncing back but that is fine. Leave to rise again somewhere warm, drizzle with olive oil and then, using your fingertips this time, squish the dough towards the edges of your baking tray once more, trying to keep an even thickness.

Peel the potatoes and slice them 2mm thick. Scatter some of the nigella seeds and a few of the rosemary sprigs on top of the focaccia, then lay the potato slices over the dough in

15g fresh yeast or a 7g
   sachet of dried yeast
600ml tepid water
1kg unbleached strong
   white bread flour,
   plus extra for dusting
20g table salt
100ml light olive oil,
   plus extra for drizzling
2 large potatoes
2 tsp nigella (black onion)
   seeds
a decent handful of
   rosemary sprigs
Maldon salt or other
   flaky sea salt

overlapping rows. Scatter the remaining nigella seeds and
rosemary on top and press the potato slices into the dough,
again using your fingertips. Leave to rise for 15 minutes,
then sprinkle with some sea salt and another good slosh of oil.
Place in an oven preheated to 200°C/Gas Mark 6 and bake for
15 minutes. Reduce the temperature to 180°C/Gas Mark 4 and
bake for a further 30 minutes or so. The focaccia should sound
hollow when you tap it underneath. Remove from the oven,
slide on to a wire rack and leave to cool.

SUMAC AND QUINOA LAVOSH

I am addicted to this thin crisp bread, our version of a lavosh from Armenia and Iran. The perfection of its salted, buttery, tangy crunch lures me into the pastry kitchen day after day at The Modern Pantry, and I am not alone! Lavosh is a little messy to make but you will quickly get the hang of it and will be delighted you persevered. Eat alone or serve with, well, anything!

Sift the flour into a bowl and add the quinoa, poppy and fennel seeds, salt and sugar. Whisk the milk and melted butter together, add to the dry ingredients and mix thoroughly with a wooden spoon until the dough becomes elastic (you could also make it in a food mixer). This is a very wet dough, so don't expect it to form a ball. Cover with cling film and leave to rest in the fridge for 20 minutes.

Scoop out a large handful of the dough on to a baking sheet lined with a silicone baking mat or a sheet of baking parchment – I highly recommend a mat, as it makes the process far quicker and easier. Oil your hands and flatten the dough out as much as you can, then generously douse it with oil. Using a rolling pin, roll it out as thinly as you can, to a maximum of 1–2mm thick. If the rolling pin sticks, add more oil. Don't worry about using too much oil, as this helps give the delightful crunch and bubble effect that occurs when you bake it, and don't worry about the odd hole either. If you somehow manage to make a massive tear, just squish some more dough in and keep rolling. If any dough goes over the edges of the mat, scrape it up and add it back to the dough in the bowl. This is a very forgiving recipe!

Once the dough is rolled, sprinkle it liberally with sumac and sparingly with sea salt. Drizzle over a little more oil for good measure, then bake in an oven preheated to 180°C/Gas Mark 4 for 7–10 minutes. The lavosh should be golden all over, with the odd darker patch. Remove from the oven and leave to cool, then break into chunks to serve. Any leftover dough will live quite happily in your fridge for up to a week. If you want uniform shapes, use a blunt knife to cut it up. Blunt is important so as not to slash your precious silicone mat!

240g plain flour
200g cooked quinoa
1 tsp poppy seeds
3 tsp fennel seeds
1 tsp table salt
¼ tsp sugar
330ml milk
50g unsalted butter, melted
vegetable oil for rolling out and drizzling
sumac for sprinkling
Maldon salt or other flaky sea salt

SPICED BEETROOT CAKE WITH SOUR GRAPES

This recipe is brilliant, not only because it is truly delicious but also for its simplicity and versatility. Try using other root vegetables, such as parsnips or carrots, and exchange the roast grapes for pineapple or rum-soaked raisins. Try different nuts or don't use them at all.

The batter works brilliantly in smaller tins, such as the fluted bundt tins I used for the photo or even muffin tins. Whatever you use, make sure you butter and sugar them well and that you don't fill them more than three-quarters full. Oh, and remember to reduce the baking time.

Sift the flour, cinnamon, star anise and bicarbonate of soda into a bowl. In another bowl, whisk the sugar with the oil, eggs and orange zest. Stir in the grated beetroot, roast grapes and toasted pecans, then fold in the sifted dry ingredients.

Butter (or oil, if you want to keep the recipe dairy-free) a round 20cm cake tin and dust with demerara sugar. Pour in the cake mixture and bake in an oven preheated to 160°C/Gas Mark 3 for 25 minutes, until a skewer inserted into the middle of the cake comes out clean. Remove from the oven and place on a wire rack to cool for 15 minutes, then remove from the tin and leave to cool completely.

For the icing, mix the icing sugar and lemon juice together until smooth. Drizzle it over the cooled cake.

SERVES 10
150g self-raising flour
1 tsp ground cinnamon
1½ tsp ground star anise
¼ tsp bicarbonate of soda
150g soft brown sugar
125ml vegetable oil
2 large eggs
grated zest of 1 orange
135g beetroot, grated
100g Pomegranate Molasses Roast Grapes (see page 56) or see above
60g pecan nuts, toasted
demerara sugar for dusting

For the lemon drizzle icing:
185g icing sugar, sifted
2 tbsp lemon juice

BANANA, COCONUT AND SAFFRON UPSIDE-DOWN CAKE

Line a 20cm springform cake tin with baking parchment. Put the white sugar and water in a pan and bring to the boil, stirring to dissolve the sugar. Continue to boil until you have a light caramel, then pour it into the base of the cake tin. Arrange the bananas cut-side down on top. You may have to cut them into shorter lengths so that they fit.

Mix the saffron with the white wine and leave to infuse for 20 minutes or so, then whisk with the vegetable oil, coconut milk and vanilla extract. Beat the eggs and caster sugar together for 30 seconds. Sift the flour and baking powder together, then stir them into the eggs and sugar along with the dessicated coconut and liquids. Beat for 1 minute, then pour into the cake tin.

Place in the centre of an oven preheated to 180°C/Gas Mark 4 and bake for 40 minutes or so, until a skewer inserted into the centre comes out clean. Transfer to a wire rack and leave for 5 minutes, then spring open the tin and remove the side. Invert the cake on a plate, very carefully remove the base of the tin and peel off the paper. Leave to cool completely.

SERVES 10

200g white sugar
80ml water
3–4 bananas, halved
  lengthways
a decent pinch of
  saffron strands
125ml white wine
250ml vegetable oil
125ml coconut milk,
  preferably including
  the extra-thick creamy
  stuff that sticks to the
  lid of the tin
2 tsp vanilla extract
4 eggs
400g caster sugar
225g plain flour
2½ tsp baking powder
100g desiccated coconut

ORANGE CAKE

This is another delight from my childhood. Mum would make this for us on birthdays and other special occasions. The finesse of this cake lies in the raw juice, which gives it a very light, fresh citrus flavour, and the zest, which ends up as a semi-crystallised coating on the top of the cake. It must be made a day in advance to allow the flavour and moisture to spread evenly and the texture to develop.

Cream the butter and 250g of the sugar together until light and fluffy, then beat in the eggs one by one. Sift in the flour and baking powder and gently but thoroughly fold them in with a large metal spoon. Spoon the mixture into a well-buttered 18cm ring mould (fluted, if you have one), place in a cold oven, then turn the heat on to 180°C/Gas Mark 4. Bake for 1 hour or until a skewer inserted in the centre comes out clean. Meanwhile, combine the orange and lemon juice and zest with the remaining sugar, stir until dissolved and then set aside.

Remove the cake from the oven and leave it to stand in its tin for 5 minutes. Turn it out and leave for a further 5 minutes. Carefully and slowly spoon the juice and sugar mixture over the cake, making sure you allow time for it to soak in. When the cake is completely cold, store in an airtight container until the following day. Serve with dollops of softly whipped cream, or with crème fraîche or natural yoghurt.

SERVES 8
250g unsalted butter, softened plus extra for greasing
400g caster sugar
3 eggs
250g plain flour
2 tsp baking powder
juice and grated zest of 1 large orange
juice and grated zest of 1 large lemon
softly whipped cream, crème fraîche or natural yoghurt, to serve

COCOA, CARDAMOM AND MACADAMIA NUT COOKIES

These biscuits are similar to shortbread, my favourite biscuit of all time. They are slightly bitter from the cocoa, and have a delicate hint of cardamom, which I love.

Beat the butter and sugar together until light and fluffy, then gradually beat in the egg, followed by the melted chocolate. Sift the dry ingredients together and fold them in, followed by the macadamia nuts. If the dough is too soft to handle, chill it for 20 minutes or so, until it is manageable, then roll it into 16 balls. If you like, you can freeze some at this stage; otherwise arrange them 5cm apart on baking trays lined with baking parchment and place in an oven preheated to 150°C/Gas Mark 2. Bake for 15 minutes, until just firm, then carefully transfer to a wire rack to cool.

SERVES 16

80g unsalted butter
175g soft brown sugar
1 egg, lightly beaten
200g dark chocolate, melted
110g plain flour
40g good-quality cocoa powder
1 tsp bicarbonate of soda
1 tsp ground cardamom
½ tsp salt
150g macadamia nuts, lightly toasted and coarsely chopped

GINGER CRUNCH

I have included this Kiwi classic because it has to be my all-time favourite slice. It couldn't be easier to make and I guarantee it will be devoured in a jiffy!

Sift the flour, cornflour, sugar, ground ginger, baking powder and salt into the bowl of an electric mixer, then add the diced butter. Using the paddle attachment, mix on medium speed until everything comes together. Press the dough evenly into an 11 x 34cm baking tin lined with baking parchment. Place in an oven preheated to 160°C/Gas Mark 3 and bake for 20 minutes.

About 5 minutes before the shortbread base is cooked, make the icing: combine all the ingredients in a small pan and heat gently, stirring constantly, until the butter has melted.

Pour the hot icing over the shortbread base as soon as it comes out of the oven. Cut into slices whilst still warm, then leave to cool completely. Ginger crunch really is best eaten the day it is made, but it will keep for up to four days in an airtight container. That is, if you don't tell anyone you made it!

MAKES ABOUT 12 SLICES
150g plain flour
25g cornflour
100g caster sugar
1 tsp ground ginger
¼ tsp baking powder
a pinch of salt
100g cold unsalted
   butter, diced

For the icing:
150g icing sugar
115g unsalted butter,
   diced
3 tbsp golden syrup
4 tsp ground ginger

GREEN TEA SCONES WITH GOOSEBERRY AND VANILLA COMPOTE

I love the grassy, savoury aroma of green tea powder, or matcha, and it happens to work particularly well in scones. You don't have to serve them with gooseberry compote – any tart jam or compote will do – but for me cream, clotted or whipped, is a must.

I have given instructions for making the scones using a food processor as I think this yields the best results but if you don't have one or prefer to make them by hand, please do. Just remember that the secret to successful scones is minimal handling and a fairly wet dough.

Besides going brilliantly with the scones, the compote is very good with meringues, vanilla ice cream or even on toast. It will keep for 2 weeks in an airtight container in the fridge.

First make the compote. Slit the vanilla pod open lengthwise and scrape out the seeds. Put the pod and seeds in a pan with the gooseberries, sugar and lemon juice. Bring to the boil, then cover the pan, reduce the heat to low and simmer for 5 minutes or so, until the gooseberries are just tender but mostly still hold their shape. Remove from the heat and leave to cool completely before serving.

For the scones, sift the flour, green tea powder, baking powder and salt into a food processor. Add the sugar and butter and pulse until the mixture resembles fine crumbs. Tip into a bowl, then add the buttermilk or milk and mix to form a dough, being careful not to overwork.

Lightly dust a work surface with flour, turn the dough out on to it and flatten to about 2.5cm thick. Cut into 12 squares with a knife, or use a pastry cutter if you prefer, and transfer to a baking sheet. Brush with milk, sprinkle over some sugar and place in an oven preheated to 220°C/Gas Mark 7. Bake for 10–12 minutes, until golden brown.

SERVES 12
400g self-raising flour
2 tsp green tea powder
½ tsp baking powder
¼ tsp salt
80g caster sugar
80g unsalted butter, diced
300ml buttermilk or whole milk
a little extra milk for brushing
granulated or demerara sugar for sprinkling

For the gooseberry and vanilla compote:
1 vanilla pod
500g gooseberries
100g white sugar
a squeeze of lemon juice

MEDJOOL DATE AND ORANGE SCONES

For those of you to whom green tea scones do not appeal, how about Medjool date and orange? I made these recently in New Zealand, with my beautiful niece and nephew, Francesca and Max, whom I love and adore above all others. They were devoured within minutes!

Sift the flour and salt into a food processor. Add the sugar, butter and orange zest and pulse until the mixture resembles fine crumbs. Tip into a bowl, then add the dates and buttermilk or milk. Mix to form a dough, being careful not to overwork.

Lightly dust a work surface with flour, turn the dough out on to it and flatten to about 2.5cm thick. Cut into 12 squares with a knife or use a pastry cutter, if you prefer, and transfer to a baking sheet. Brush with milk, sprinkle over some sugar or and place in an oven preheated to 220°C/Gas Mark 7. Bake for 10–12 minutes, until golden brown.

SERVES 12
400g self-raising flour
¼ tsp salt
1½ tbsp caster sugar
80g unsalted butter, diced
grated zest of 2 oranges
150g Medjool dates,
  pitted and chopped
300ml buttermilk or
  whole milk
a little extra milk for brushing
granulated or demerara
  sugar for sprinkling

My Pantry Stockists

My Pantry

Life as a chef without access to spices is no life at all. They are and always have been an essential part of the process. What would a simple béchamel sauce be without the addition of freshly grated nutmeg, or a juicy rib-eye steak without a twist of black pepper? Dull.

I love the endless aroma and flavour possibilities that spices offer. The opportunity to transform a roast sweet potato with a sprinkling of ground fenugreek or to enhance a classic vinaigrette with the earthy nuttiness of toasted black mustard seeds gives me joy every day.

At The Modern Pantry, we buy whole spices rather than ground ones where possible. They remain fresh longer this way, which in turn means a more potent flavour. Freshness is key, so regularly check the use-by dates of the spices in your cupboard. If they have expired, bin them and buy some more.

I don't really enjoy buying spices from supermarkets. The range tends to be limited and the less commonly used ones can sometimes be stale. Try shopping at a local Indian, Greek, Turkish or Chinese store, if you have one. These are cultures that use spices daily in their cooking and charge accordingly. Often you will get twice as much for half the price and without the unnecessary packaging. Alternatively you can purchase all the spices listed below over the internet – have a look at the list on page 247 for some suggested suppliers.

I also recommend purchasing a spice grinder (we use a coffee grinder) or a mortar and pestle, so that you can buy whole seeds or quills and grind them yourself.

As well as spices this section also gives you a guide to some of the more quirky or unusual ingredients I have used throughout the book. Like the spices most can be purchased on-line (see page 247). They are all ingredients I like having in my pantry and I hope they will be making an appearance in your pantry soon too!

Aleppo chilli flakes
Aleppo chillies come from the place of the same name in Northern Syria. The whole chillies are salted, semi-dried and then flaked and rubbed with oil, yielding a vibrant, rich colour and an oily texture not dissimilar to Urfa chilli flakes (see page 241). They are reasonably mild, with a sweetness you don't expect in a chilli, making them incredibly versatile. Use them in place of ordinary dried chillies or sprinkled over a perfectly ripe mango with a wedge of lime. I am addicted to them.

Amchur powder
A tangy, fruity powder made from dried green or unripe mangoes. It is used as a souring agent, like tamarind, in curries, soups, chutneys and marinades, where it also acts as a tenderiser. I like to sprinkle amchur powder on potatoes or parsnips before roasting them, or add it to a salad dressing as an alternative to lemon juice.

Assam
Indigenous to Malaysia, this fruit is used as a souring agent as well as for preserving fish and meat. It looks like a small green-and-yellow pumpkin, and the rind and flesh are dried and preserved. Both fruit and leaves, which are sold as tea, are said to have health benefits, ranging from aiding digestion and weight loss to boosting energy and general mood. Try adding a piece to a laksa or stew.

Bee pollen

You can find bee pollen in any decent health-food shop or
buy it online. As well as having untold health benefits, which
I will leave you to discover, it has a distinctive musky, honeyish
flavour that I love. I have used it in a baked ricotta dish (see
page 76) but you could also try adding it to a risotto or whisking
it into a honey and lemon vinaigrette.

Cassava

Also called yucca or manioc, cassava is a tropical plant native
to Central and South America. The roots are either boiled or
fried, and are also turned into flour and tapioca (very similar
to sago), and even beer.

Chipotle chilli flakes and powder

Chipotles are smoked jalapeño chillies, rather hot, although
not quite a bird's eye. They have a wonderful smoky, savoury
flavour that is perfect for lifting a stew or soup.

Curry leaves

These look like very small bay leaves and are an essential
ingredient in South Indian curries. They have a slightly nutty,
earthy taste which I find goes well with most things. They
should be fried in oil first to release their full flavour and aroma.
Don't be afraid to buy a large bunch when you come across them
as they freeze very well. I don't recommend buying dried curry
leaves as they seem to lose all their flavour.

Dried shrimps

You can pick up these small, sweet, sun-dried shrimps at any
Asian supermarket. They are added to many dishes, ranging
from sambals to gumbos and dim sum. Like fish sauce, they
impart 'umami', or savouriness, to your cooking.

Fish sauce

Also known as nam pla, amongst many other names, this
pungent, salty liquid is made from fermented fish and is a
brilliant seasoning. It is added to the dressing for the classic
Thai beef salad and is often used in laksas, curries and the
like, adding another layer of flavour as well as salt. Go easy
on it though, as the taste is very concentrated.

HIJIKI

Hijiki
This seaweed is often used in Japanese cooking – wakame is another favourite. Available dried at any Japanese supermarket, it is easy to rehydrate and adds great texture and flavour to any dish. Try adding it to braised lentils with a little butter and parsley or tossing it through a salad.

Kalamansi (or calamansi) lime
Also known as sour orange, this is a small citrus fruit with green skin and orange flesh. It is thought to be a cross between a tangerine or mandarin and a kumquat. The juice is extracted by crushing the whole fruit, yielding a wonderful, sherbet-flavoured, mango-coloured liquid. Try using it in place of lime juice. It also makes a refreshing spritzer.

Labneh
Labneh is a fresh cheese made by straining yoghurt through a cloth or filter – often a muslin – to remove the whey. The result has a texture somewhere between a Greek yoghurt and a soft cheese. Preserved in oil it lasts for a good few weeks stored in

your fridge. Try rolling it in different herbs and spices, such
as rosemary or sumac, or mixing fruits or pickles through it
for texture and flavour. I like to mix it with chopped umeboshi
plums or finely diced apple. You could also try flavouring the
cheese itself as I have done in my recipe for Coconut Labneh
(see page 112).

Lemongrass

I love the refreshing fragrance and versatility of this grass,
which can be used equally well in sweet and savoury dishes and
makes an excellent cup of tea. It freezes brilliantly so don't be
put off if you have to buy a bunch, which is how it is usually sold.

Lotus root

This is, in fact, not the root of the lotus plant but the stem,
which rises from the bed of the pond and keeps the plant afloat.
Once peeled, the rhizome can be pickled (see page 28), boiled,
deep-fried, stir-fried, stuffed and more. Although I don't find its
flavour particularly thrilling *au naturel*, I love the texture, and
it looks beautiful dyed golden or red adorning a plate, or sliced
thinly and fried until golden and crisp. Sprinkle a little amchur
powder and fine sea salt over the lotus for a flavour boost.

Mirin

A sweet cooking wine used prolifically in Japanese cuisine.
It is made from glutinous rice that has been steamed and mixed
with koji (steamed rice that has had a mould spore cultivated
into it) and shochu, a Japanese distilled spirit.

Muscatel vinegar

A deliciously sweet vinegar made with the wine from the
Muscatel grape. Make sure you buy a decent-quality one,
use as you would white wine vinegar or cider vinegar and
be prepared for a pleasant surprise.

Palm sugar

A soft brown sugar from Southeast Asia taken from the sap
of various palms, including the date, sago and coconut palms.
It has a rich toffeeish flavour and can be pale or dark, hard,
soft or even liquid. The main reason for the variation is that
the manufacture of palm sugar is a small cottage industry and
therefore not homogenous: cultivators use different techniques

which bring different results. Palm sugar is sold in a variety
of shapes depending on what vessel the reduced sap has been
poured into to set. Bamboo tubes, coconut shells and plastic
bags are just three of the possibilities.

Pandan leaves

Known as the vanilla of Southeast Asia, pandan imparts a
distinctive aroma and flavour to savoury and sweet dishes
alike. Its taste is very hard to describe, as it isn't really like
anything else, but it has a slightly sweet, musky jasmine-rice
aroma to it. Not very clear. You'll just have to go and buy some!
It freezes well and, besides using it in the Borlotti Bean, Pandan
and Vanilla Stew on page 122 or the Coconut and Pandan Duck
Leg Curry on page 164, you could try crushing a leaf or two
and cooking it in a custard or adding it to a pot of tea.

Panko crumbs

Panko is a type of breadcrumb made by the Japanese. It is
particularly light and fluffy as the crumbs are made from only
the soft part of the bread. The crumbs are used for coating
foods before frying; they give a particularly good crunch which
is why they are often used in place of ordinary breadcrumbs.

Plantain

A variety of banana that is only ever used in cooking, never
eaten raw. Like eating bananas plantain comes in many shades
but here in the UK it is mostly only available green or yellow,
whether ripe or unripe. Plantain is used in much the same way
as any starchy vegetable – it can be boiled, fried, roasted or
added to soups and stews.

Plum wine

See Umeshu

Pomegranate molasses

I have come to love this rich, sweet and sour molasses from
the Middle East so much that I feel rather anxious when we
occasionally run out of it at the restaurant. Its versatility is
inspiring. I use it in dressings, in marinades for poultry and
lamb, drizzled on a fresh fruit salad or to bring a flat beetroot
soup to life. It is readily available in most Mediterranean and
Middle Eastern stores and in some delis and large supermarkets.

Salsify

Sago

Sago is a starch extracted from the stems of various palms, including the sago palm. It is sold as flour and used as a thickening agent or as sago pearls. I am a particular fan of the soft but chewy texture of the pearls and use them whenever I can in both savoury and sweet preparations. Recently I have boiled them then mixed them with squid ink and crustacea oil to create a fake caviar.

Salsify

Salsify, also known as *oyster vegetable* due to its delicate oyster-like flavour, is a root vegetable. I tend to find its flavour more akin to white asparagus however so don't be put off by the oyster reference if you have an aversion to them. Although salsify is not all that easy to come by, when one does it is definitely worth the purchase. Its black, sandy, soil-covered skins are easily washed and peeled revealing long creamy white fingers which can be prepared as you would any other root vegetable. Try adding to stews or steaming and serving with butter like potatoes, blanching and pan frying with capers and parsley, or roasting with fresh curry leaves and turmeric, mustard seeds and garlic for example.

Salted yuzu juice

The yuzu fruit originated in China but is used most extensively in Japanese cuisine. Its delicate flavour, which is less acidic than that of lemon or lime juice, enhances everything from meat, poultry and fish to vegetable and noodle dishes. Try adding some to an avocado salsa or sprinkling a little over stone fruit before roasting. Add it sparingly, though, as a little goes a long way.

Shaoxing

As well as being a region in China shaoxing is one of the most famous traditional Chinese fermented wines. It is made from rice and is similar to a dry sherry in flavour. It can be drunk and is widely used as a marinade for meat and fish. Try adding some to a stock next time you make one.

Shichimi

Also known as shichimi togarashi, this is a popular Japanese table condiment used to give a bit of a kick to a dish. The mix contains seven ingredients, typically ground red chilli pepper,

TAMARILLO

Szechuan pepper, roasted orange peel, black and white sesame seeds, hemp seed, ground ginger and nori.

Sorrel
A soft herb with a sour lemony flavour which is used for many different culinary purposes. Try adding it to salsas or soups or simply tearing up the leaves and tossing them through a fresh garden salad.

Star anise
Indigenous to China this small, star-shaped spice is very similar to anise in its flavour (although they are unrelated) and is one that I use every day in my kitchen. It goes very well with meats such as pork and duck as well as with sweet things such as chocolate and ice cream.

Sumac
This spice is made from the ground red fruits of the sumac plant and is used prolifically in Middle Eastern, Arabic and

Turkish cuisines. It is a deep maroon or purple colour and has a wonderful lemony flavor. Try sprinkling it over potatoes just before you roast them or adding to soup for an extra layer of flavour.

Tamarillo

These red or yellow egg shaped fruits are native to South America but grow prolifically in New Zealand where they are also known as tree tomatoes. They are rather tart but are delicious. Try halving them lengthways and roasting them sprinkled with sugar and star anise, or dicing the flesh and using it as the base of a salsa for beef or venison.

Tamarind

This is a sweet and sour condiment made from the pulp of ripe seedpods from the tamarind tree. It is commonly used in many countries from Egypt to Mexico, Africa to Asia, and has multiple uses both medicinal and gastronomic. You can buy tamarind as a ready-to-use paste or in a sticky, dense block of pulp and seed, which is very easily transformed into a paste. The latter has a superior flavour, but if you are short of time the ready-to-use option is perfectly adequate.

Thai basil

A wonderfully pungent south-east Asian herb with liquorice and anise overtones that I love and use regularly in my cooking. It is available from most Asian supermarkets and is also now being grown as a micro leaf by an English company called WOW. Although these are not as potent as the fully-grown leaves from Thailand they are produced locally and do taste pretty good.

Tomatillos

Tomatillos are small, green, tomato-like fruits wrapped in a papery husk like their relative, the Cape gooseberry. The flavour is slightly tart, and adds a refreshing zing to salsas and salads. It is particularly good with white meats.

Tonka beans

Dried tonka beans have a sweet, almond-like flavour and are often used as an alternative to vanilla, as well as in soaps, tobacco and perfumes. It is a particularly good flavouring for desserts. Try infusing the milk for a panna cotta with tonka

beans instead of vanilla, or make the Tonka Bean and Chilli
Truffles on page 206. I have also flavoured a celeriac mash
with it, which was delicious. Get creative!

Turmeric

This comes in two forms, fresh and ground. My preference
for this remarkably fragrant and colourful spice is fresh, but
dried powdered turmeric is perfectly adequate. If using fresh,
I suggest wearing gloves, as the oily yellow pigment stains
quickly. It will wash out in time!

Umeboshi

Japanese pickled plums, though they are apparently more
closely related to apricots, are traditionally served as a side
dish to a main meal, as a filling in rice balls and may also
accompany a cup of green tea. As well as aiding digestion
they are also said to reduce nausea including nausea resulting
from a hangover. I have yet to test that theory! They are super-
sour, savoury and salty and I love them. Try blitzing the flesh
of 4 plums into 100g of butter with a clove of garlic then use
to fry fish or melt over potatoes, or as you would garlic butter
in bread. I have also added them to a caramel sauce with Urfa
chilli flakes which was quite delicious.

Umeshu

A Japanese plum liqueur, also known as plum wine, made by
steeping unripe ume fruit in shochu (a clear distilled spirit)
and sugar. I love it. Try soaking prunes in it with some ground
toasted caraway seeds – great with pork.

Urfa chilli flakes

This moderately hot, purplish chilli from the Turkish town
of Urfa is another firm favourite at The Modern Pantry and is
used in many of the recipes in this book. The peppers are picked
and cut, then go through a process of being dried in the sun by
day, then wrapped tightly and 'sweated' at night. This infuses
the flesh with any remaining moisture in the chilli and the
end-result is a superb oily texture, an earthy, raisin-like flavour
and a smoky aroma. I love them and, as with Aleppo chilli
flakes (see page 235), use them in practically everything.
Try sprinkling them on grilled meats just before serving,
or even adding them to the caramel of a tarte Tatin. The
possibilities really are endless.

VERJUS

Verjus

Meaning green juice, this condiment is made by pressing
unripe grapes. It has been around since Roman times and,
although once widely used, is less well-known now. Use as
you would lemon juice in dressings and sauces, or to deglaze
a pan after frying meat.

Wasabi tobiko

This is the roe of a flying fish that has been steeped in wasabi.
The roe is very small and crunchy, so when you eat it you get
bursts of heat popping in your mouth – they're like wasabi peas
from the sea!

Wattleseed

An Australian bush food. Seeds from the Acacia tree are
harvested then roasted and ground to make wattleseed. Its
flavour is reminiscent of coffee, hazelnuts and chocolate and
it can be used in both sweet and savoury dishes. It is fantastic
folded through meringues before baking but it also works when
sprinkled over vegetables such as parsnips or butternut squash
before roasting. It would be ideal in the Muscovado Meringues
on page 192 – simply mix a tablespoon of wattlesed with the
muscovado sugar before folding through the meringue mixture.

White miso

This traditional Japanese seasoning is available as a paste or
powder. High in protein and rich in minerals and vitamins, it is
made by fermenting soya beans, barley or rice with salt. There
are many varieties of miso, all with subtle differences in flavour
and texture.

   At The Modern Pantry we always have a stock of white miso
to hand. We use it daily to marinate onglet steak (see page 181),
one of our signature dishes. Moromi miso, a barley-based miso,
is another favourite we use to spread on fish or to add texture
and punch to a crisp raw salad.

STOCKISTS

www.thespicery.com
Specialising in spices, herbs, chillies, seeds, and flowers, thespicery.com stocks a wide range of specialist ingredients, including, Aleppo chilli flakes, amchur, curry leaves, chipotle, sumac, tamarind, Urfa chilli flakes and wattleseed.

www.japancentre.com
The on-line oulet of the London-based Japanese shop which sells food, kitchenware and more. Look out for dried shrimps, hijiki, lotus root, mirin, Panko crumbs, yuzu juice, shichimi, umeboshi and umeshu.

www.japanesefoodshop.co.uk
Another Japanese stockist offering a wide range of authentic ingredients.

www.thai-food-online.co.uk
A Thai and Asian on-line supermarket that stocks essential ingredients for cooking authentic Thai dishes at home. You'll find palm sugar, pandan leaves and Thai basil.

www.coolchile.co.uk
Cool Chile Co specialises in Mexican dried chillies and other useful ingredients to make Mexican food. Products available include tamarind and tomatillos.

INDEX

ACKNOWLEDGEMENTS

First and foremost thank you so much Sarah Lavelle and Imogen Fortes for taking a punt and commissioning me to write this book. I was/am still thrilled to pieces and it has been an absolute pleasure to work with you both.

Thank you Kate Sclater, Tim Balaam and Rose Reeves of Hyperkit for coming up with the beautiful images that ARE The Modern Pantry and for designing such a beautiful, timeless and elegant book.

Thank you Chris Terry and Danny for capturing the essence of The Modern Pantry so perfectly on film and for your utter enthusiasm throughout this project.

Thank you Dad and Joan for your tireless edits, for asking so many questions, for testing the odd recipe and for always being there.

Thank you Mum for your eternal encouragement and love and thank you to the rest of my family, past and present, just for being.

An enormous thank you to my brilliant team at The Modern Pantry who have all at some point played a part in the creation of this book, in particular Antonello Bux, Candi Giacchetti, John Hurley, Robert Mcleary, Elaine Murzi, Dougal Spratt and Lizzy Stables, the backbone of The Modern Pantry, thank you for your endless patience and support.

And finally thank you to my dear, dear friends Sarah Conway, Bill Knott, Sue Lewis, Elaine Murzi, Sholto Pridgeon, Joanna Salmond Chang and Giancarlo Vatteroni without whose seemingly boundless love and encouragement The Modern Pantry might not exist at all.

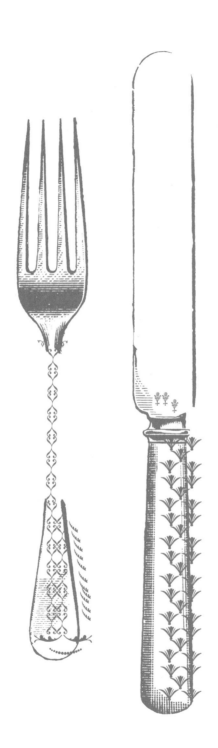

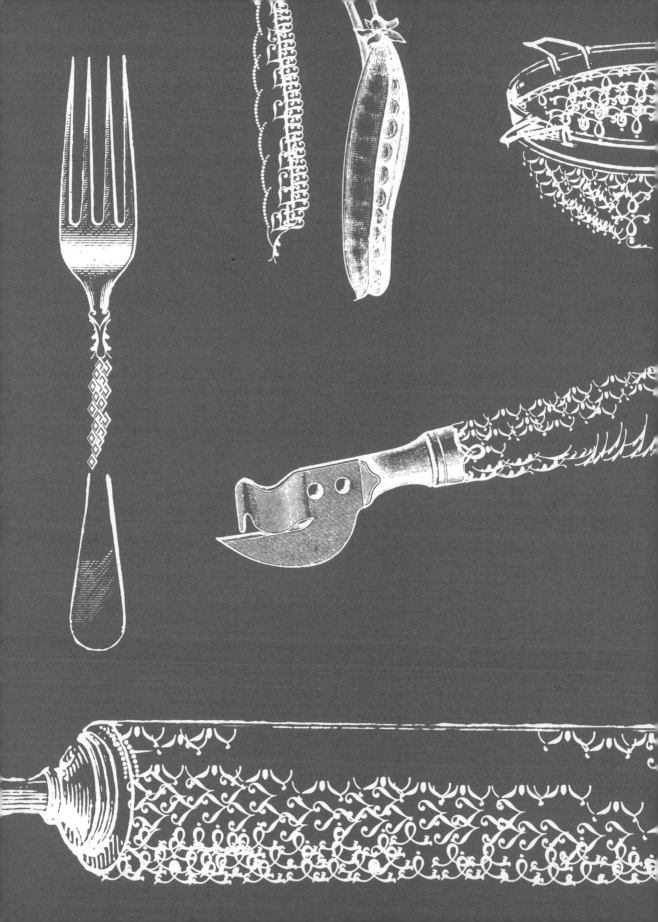